File on GORKY

Compiled by Cynthia Marsh

Methuen Drama

A Methuen Drama Book

First published in Great Britain 1993
by Methuen Drama,
an imprint of Reed Consumer Books Ltd.,
Michelin House, 81 Fulham Road, London SW3 6RB,
and Auckland, Melbourne, Singapore, and Toronto,
and distributed in the United States of America by HEB Inc.,
361 Hanover Street, Portsmouth, New Hampshire 03801-3959

ISBN 413 65060 X

A CIP catalogue record for this book
is available at the British Library

Typeset in 9/10 Times by
L. Anderson Typesetting,
Woodchurch, Kent TN26 3TB

Printed in Great Britain
by Cox and Wyman Ltd.,
Cardiff Road, Reading

Front cover photograph of Gorky
is reproduced by courtesy of
the Society for Cultural Relations
with the USSR

Contents

Abbreviations

Books

PSS   M. Gor'kii, *Pol'noe sobranie sochinenii*,
   Moscow, 1968-76. [*Complete Collected Works*,
   of which Volume VII (Moscow, 1970) and
   Volume XIII (Moscow, 1972) are the main
   volumes cited. Location and date of publication
   given on first citation only.]

SS   M. Gor'kii, *Sobranie sochinenii*, Moscow,
   1949-66. [*Collected Works*.]

Sob. soch.   *Sobranie sochinenii* [*Collected Works*,
   by other writers].

Theatres

MAT   Moscow Art Theatre.

BDT   Bol'shoi dramaticheskii teatr [Large
   Dramatic Theatre], Leningrad.

MGSPS   Moskovskii gorodskoi sovet
   professional'nykh soiuzov [Theatre of the
   Moscow Soviet of Trade Unions, 1930-38.
   Before 1938 known as MGSPS, after 1938 as
   Theatre of the Moscow Soviet].

RSC   Royal Shakespeare Company.

The theatre is, by its nature, an ephemeral art: yet it is a daunting task to track down the newspaper reviews, or contemporary statements from the writer or his director, which are often all that remain to help us recreate some sense of what a particular production was like. This series is therefore intended to make readily available a selection of the comments that the critics made about the plays of leading modern dramatists at the time of their production — and to trace, too, the course of each writer's own views about his work and his world.

In addition to combining a uniquely convenient source of such elusive *documentation*, the 'Writer-Files' series also assembles the *information* necessary for readers to pursue further their interest in a particular writer or work. Variations in quantity between one writer's output and another's, differences in temperament which make some readier than others to talk about their work, and the variety of critical response, all mean that the presentation and balance of material shifts between one volume and another: but we have tried to arrive at a format for the series which will nevertheless enable users of one volume readily to find their way around any other.

Section 1, 'A Brief Chronology', provides a quick conspective overview of each playwright's life and career. *Section 2* deals with the plays themselves, arranged chronologically in the order of their composition: information on first performances, major revivals, and publication is followed by a brief synopsis (for quick reference set in slightly larger, italic type), then by a representative selection of the critical response, and of the dramatist's own comments on the play and its theme.

Section 3 offers concise guidance to each writer's work in non-dramatic forms, while *Section 4*, 'The Writer on His Work', brings together comments from the playwright himself on more general matters of construction, opinion, and artistic development. Finally, *Section 5* provides a bibliographical guide to other primary and secondary sources of further reading, among which full details will be found of works cited elsewhere under short titles, and of collected editions of the plays — but not of individual titles, particulars of which will be found with the other factual data in Section 2.

The 'Writer-Files' hope by striking this kind of balance between information and a wide range of opinion to offer 'companions' to the study of major playwrights in the modern repertoire — not in that dangerous pre-digested fashion which can too readily quench the desire to read the plays themselves, nor so prescriptively as to allow any single line of approach to predominate, but rather to encourage readers to form their own judgements of the plays in a wide-ranging context.

Maxim Gorky's place in the Russian as distinct from the former Soviet theatre is in process of painful reassessment. To have been neglected as old-fashioned in the creative and relatively open artistic environment of the 1920s, and then held up as a model of socialist realism amidst the oppression of the 1930s, is scarcely a recommendation in the present political climate. And yet Gorky wrote largely, almost obsessively, of those most capitalist of institutions, the family and the small business – a preoccupation underlined by the inclusiveness of this *Writer-File*, as earlier by the succession of RSC productions of the lesser-known plays, which revealed *The Lower Depths* to have been, if still his masterpiece, uncharacteristic in its chosen milieu.

Thus, although the bourgeois focus of Gorky's plays was declared by one respected Soviet critic (as here recorded on page 55) to have been 'a reflection of class conflicts', those conflicts today seem as rooted in the perceptions of Freud as of Marx. As one of his leading translators into English, Jeremy Brooks, points out on page 32, this helps to account for the favourable response towards the RSC productions of their British audiences, who are more comfortably attuned than their European neigh-bours to appreciating political conflict within the familial microcosm than as a matter of 'whether you live or die tomorrow'.

Increasingly, the strong man in Gorky's various family groups turns out to be a woman – sometimes overweening in an almost Strindbergian fashion, but more often with a force of will that is outwardly-directed in its fierce protection of the security of the home, and of its economic under-pinning. Then again, in *The Old Man* especially, there are qualities (as here discussed on page 78) that are recognisably Ibsenesque – notably Gorky's sense of the determining effects of past actions upon present behaviour, and his increasing inclination to probe the individual rather than the collective psyche.

Such associations are helpful in so far as they direct our thinking out-wards from the more commonplace comparisons with Chekhov – whose families seem almost English in their allusive reticence besides the Slavic implosiveness of Gorky's. Yet there is much, too, in his later charac-ters – those small businessmen eternally unfulfilled or, like Egor Bulychev, clinging to the flimsiest hopes of redemption – that relates them to the compulsive dreamers of *The Lower Depths*. No more can we finally assert of the foxy merchant Bulychev than of the vagrant Luka whether he is life-affirming or life-denying in his dreams.

Simon Trussler

1868 16 March: Aleksei Maksimovich Peshkov (Gorky's real name) born in Nizhnii Novgorod (known in this century variously as Nizhegorod and Gorky), the major town at the point where the Oka flows into the Volga. Father a boatyard carpenter.

1871 Father transferred as boatyard manager to Astrakhan, but shortly afterwards dies of cholera. Aleksei returns with mother to her parents, who own a small dye works. Graphic account of early years in first volume of his autobiography, *Childhood*.

1879 Mother dies of tuberculosis. Aleksei works in a shoe-shop as general dogsbody.

1880 Apprenticed to draftsman: treated badly, and runs away as cabin boy on Volga steamboat. Tries other professions, including icon painting, watchman at a building site, clerk. Spends spare time reading. Mixes with students, tramps, and prostitutes.

1884 Leaves for Kazan', possibly to study. Lives from hand to mouth, often taking odd jobs in docks. Mixes with students. Realizes he is unsuited to discipline of study.

1887 Working in a bakery. Feb.: death of his grandmother affects him deeply. Dec.: attempts suicide.

1888 Works among peasants at Krasnodivovo with a radical colleague. Disillusioned, wanders in the Volga region. Works for a time in Tsaritsyn (later to be known as Stalingrad and Volgograd) as a menial in railway administration. Spends free time reading. Interest in Tolstoyism. Begins to write.

1889 Makes way to Moscow to visit Tolstoy, but he is absent on pilgrimage. Returns to Nizhnii Novgorod and lives with radicals: under surveillance. Works in brewery, then for a lawyer. Contacts the writer V. G. Korolenko to show him his work: disillusioned by his comments.

1891 Sets off on journey working his way through Russia and Ukraine, mostly on foot.

1892 Encouraged to write again: 'Makar Chudra', a short story, published in Caucasus under the pseudonym of Maxim Gorky ('Bitter'). Returns to Nizhnii Novgorod. Works for lawyer again. Several short stories published

1895 Moves to Samara to work as newspaper columnist.

1896 Returns to Nizhnii Novgorod as editor. Marries E. P. Volzhina. Tuberculosis diagnosed.

1897 With help from a literary fund in Petersburg, Peshkovs leave for convalescence in Crimea. July: son Maxim born.

1898 May: arrested in Nizhnii Novgorod for previously associating with radicals. Placed under strict surveillance. First collection of short stories published in Petersburg: a sellout. Sends it to Chekhov as a token of his admiration.

1899 Publication of his first novel, *Foma Gordeev*. March: Gorky meets Chekhov in Yalta. Popularity enormous: Repin paints his portrait, and Gorky regarded as model for radical literature and politics.

1900 Speaks out against conscription of radical students. Meets Tolstoy.

1901 Joins demonstration in favour of students in Petersburg. Placed under house arrest. Radical novel *The Three of Them* published. May: daughter Ekaterina born. Nov.: allowed to go to Crimea for health. Demonstrations of support accompany him. *Philistines* in rehearsal at Moscow Art Theatre (MAT). Stays with Chekhov in Crimea for week. Visits Tolstoy.

1902 Election to Academy of Sciences cancelled following Tsar's objection. Chekhov and Korolenko resign. March: *Philistines* opens amid intense controversy while MAT on tour to Petersburg. Ordered to Arzamas. Completes *The Lower Depths*: opens in Dec., to loud acclaim.

1903 Joins Znanie publishing house. Widely popular for his work among radicals, liberals, and the reading public at large, but figure of suspicion elsewhere in establishment. Separates from wife.

1904 July: deeply affected by death of Chekhov. Nov.: premiere of *Summerfolk* at Kommissarzhevskaia's Theatre, Petersburg: denounced by the artistic elite as propaganda.

1905 Jan.: involved in events of Bloody Sunday: arrested and imprisoned for his protest. Writes *Children of the Sun* in prison. International call for his release. Sent to Riga under police surveillance. Involved in Bolshevik press. Oct.: tempestuous premiere of *Children of the Sun* (MAT). Nov.: meets Lenin, newly returned from exile.

1906 Goes to America via France with M. Andreeva, partly to escape reaction in Russia and to win support for the Bolsheviks. Enjoys international acclaim, but scandal in America when discovered Andreeva and Gorky not married. Completes novel, *The Mother*, and play, *Enemies*. Aug.: daughter dies in Russia. Nov.: premiere of *Barbarians* in Riga.

1907 Feb: premiere of *Enemies*, Berlin. Takes refuge in Italy, residing finally in Capri. Stays until 1913. Stream of political and literary visitors in these years, including Lenin.

1908 *Confession* published: reflects interest in fusion of Christianity and Marxism (referred to as 'god-building'). June: premiere of *The Last Ones*, Tashkent.

1910 Details of the death of Tolstoy appal him. Begins publication of long novel *The Life of Matvei Kozhemiakin*. Oct.: premiere of *The Eccentrics* in Petersburg and of *The Reception* in Kiev.

1911 Feb.: premiere of *Vassa Zheleznova* (first version), Moscow.

1912 Begins work on *The Zykovs*

1913 First volume of autobiographical trilogy, *Childhood*, published. Begins work on *Counterfeit Coin*. Dec.: returns to Russia under amnesty.

1915 Sets up journal *Letopis'* (*The Chronicle*): does not always follow strict Bolshevik line, to Lenin's wrath. Completes *The Old Man*.

1916 Second volume of autobiography, *In the World*, published in *Letopis'*.

1917 Founds newspaper *Novaiazhizn* (*New Life*).

1918 July: premiere of *The Zykovs*, Petrograd. *New Life* closed down on Lenin's orders. Gorky accommodates himself to Bolshevik cause.

1919 Jan.: premiere of *The Old Man*, Moscow. Intercedes with Bolsheviks on behalf of intellectuals. Organizes committee to protect Russia's cultural heritage.

1920   Separates from Andreeva in favour of M. Budberg. June: *Workaholic Slovotekov*, premiered in Petrograd, banned after four performances.

1921   Health undermined, leaves for sanatorium in Black Forest, and remains in Germany.

1923   Party to setting up journal *Beseda* (*Conversation*) in Berlin in an attempt to reconcile Soviets and emigrés. Publication of third volume of autobiography, *My Universities*.

1924   Returns to Italy. Debarred from Capri, stays in Sorrento.

1925   Publication of novel *The Artamanov Affair* in Berlin. Undertakes final novel *The Life of Klim Samgin* (unfinished at his death).

1926   Completes *Counterfeit Coin*.

1928   May: returns to Moscow for six months. Immense official and popular reception. Winters in Sorrento. Italian premiere of *Counterfeit Coin*, Rome and Naples.

1929   May, again returns to Moscow, including trip on Volga in itinerary. Oct.: returns to Sorrento in deteriorating health.

1930   Writes *Somov and the Others*.

1931   May: returns to Moscow. Highly decorated and honoured. Oct.: returns to Sorrento. Completes *Egor Bulychev and the Others*.

1932   May-Oct.: visit to Russia. Sept.: premiere of *Egor Bulychev and the Others*, Moscow, Leningrad. Completes *Dostigaev and the Others*.

1933   May: final departure from Italy for Russia. Leads life of prominent public figure, but also watched. Moscow house centre of intellectual life. Becomes spokesman for Soviet view on art and literature. Nov.: premiere of *Dostigaev and the Others*, Leningrad and Moscow.

1934   Feb: MAT premiere of *Egor Bulychev and the Others*. May: son Max dies. Aug.: chairman of first Congress of Soviet Writers.

1935   Undertakes triumphant tour on Volga. Health deteriorates. Winter in Crimea. Completes second version of *Vassa Zheleznova*.

1936   Returns to Moscow in May, and dies on 18 June.

a: Major Plays

Philistines

'Scenes in the House of Bessemenov. A Dramatic Sketch in Four Acts.'

Written: 1901. Awarded the Griboedov Prize, 1903.

First production: MAT on tour, Panaevskii Th., St Petersburg, 26 Mar. 1902; premiere in Moscow, 8 Oct. 1902 (dir. K. S. Stanislavski, V. V. Luzhskii; des. V. A. Simov; with Luzhskii as Bessemenov, O. Knipper as Elena, and V. E. Meierkhold as Petr).

Major revivals: Perm, 19 May 1902 (dir. Vronchenko-Levitskii; full version as passed for MAT); permission not granted for imperial theatres, but provincial revivals (with censor-imposed cuts) included Belostock, Vilno, Ekaterinburg, Irkutsk, Kazan', Kostroma, Krasnoiarsk, Niznii-Novgorod, Odessa, Orenburg, 1902; Saratov, 1903 (dir. N. I. Sobolschikov-Samarin, who also played Bessemenov and Teterev); Aleksandrinskii Company at the Mikhailovskii Th., 7 Apr. 1917; BDT, Leningrad, 1937 (dir. Meluzov); Malyi Th., 1946 (dir. A. D. Dikii); MAT, 1949 (dir. S. K. Blinnikov, I. M. Raevskii, M. N. Kedrov); BDT, Leningrad, 1967 (dir. G. A. Tovstonogov; with E. Lebedev as Bessemenov).

First British production: as *The Bessemenovs*, Mermaid Society at Terry's Th., 23 Apr. 1906 (tr. J. R. Crauford; dir. Edward Terry; with Herbert Grimwood as Bessemenov).

Revived: as *Middle-Class People*, Yiddish Art Th. of America, Scala Th., 17 May 1924 (dir. Maurice Schwartz); RSC at The Other Place, Stratford, 30 Mar. 1985 (dir. John Caird; with David Burke as Bessemenov, Fiona Shaw as Tatiana, and Tom Mannion as Nil).

Major European revivals: Lessing Th., Berlin, 1902; Breslau Th., 1902; Raimundtheater, 1902; Hamburg, 1902-3; Darmstadt, 1902-3; Leipzig; 1902-3; Teatro Fossati, Milan, 1903; Munich Th., 1903; Th. National, Paris, 1903; Zentral Th., Berlin, 1922 (dir. Erwin Piscator).

First published: St. Petersburg: 'Znanie', 1902.

Translations: by E. Hopkins, as *The Lower Middle Class*, in *Poet Lore*, XVII, 4 (1906); as *Smug Citizen* (Boston, 1907); as *The Petit-Bourgeois*, tr. M. Wettlin, in Gorky, *Five Plays* (Moscow, 1956), and in *Collected Works in Ten*

Volumes, Vol. IV (Moscow, 1978-80); as *The Courageous One*, adapted by M. Goldina and H. Choat (New York, 1958); as *Philistines*, tr. Dusty Hughes, from a literal translation by Helen Rappaport (Oxford, 1985).

Set in a wealthy tradesman's house at the turn of the century, Philistines *charts the break-up of the Bessemenov family, rejecting bourgeois values in favour of a working-class ethic. Bessemenov, working unceasingly at his trade of house-painter, has built himself a successful business, educated his children Petr and Tatiana well beyond his own level, and cast his adopted son Nil in his own image by apprenticing him as a mechanic in the engine yards. However, Petr has been expelled from university, and Tatiana works unhappily as a teacher. Nil, by contrast, is hardworking, energetic, and power-hungry. He claims his labour at the engine yards entitles him to a say in household decisions and to his independence. All are on a collision path. Bessemenov upbraids his children for their inactivity, driving Petr into the arms of an attractive lodger Elena. Tatiana is secretly in love with Nil, and destined in her father's mind for him. Father and daughter are devastated when Nil declares his intention to marry Polia, a seamstress and daughter of the lodger, the birdcatcher Perchikhin. Tatiana attempts to poison herself. Nil is undeterred from his departure with Polia, regarding it as an assertion of his values against those of his adopted family. Petr announces his marriage to Elena, and is forecast by another lodger Teterev, a shrewd and frequently drunk commentator on the action, to be the future inheritor not only of his father's possessions but also his attitudes. At the close the Bessemenov parents contemplate their lonely future, while Tatiana falls disconsolately over the piano keys, producing chords of jangling disharmony.*

In all honesty I will say that I don't like the play. . . . There's no poetry in it. That's what is wrong. There's a lot of noise and upset, a lot of nerve, but no fire. But I'm not going to touch it — it can go to the devil! I wrote it in eighteen days and I'm not going to spend another hour on it.

Gorky, letter to K. P. Piatnitskii, 14 or 15 Oct. 1901,
SS, Vol. 28 (Moscow, 1954), p. 180

The central figure of the play, Nil, is strongly drawn and exceptionally interesting! . . . The play engages from the very first act. . . . The role of Nil, a marvellous part, should be made two or three times longer. He should close the play and become its main character. But don't juxtapose him to Petr and Tatiana. Let him and them stand alone. . . . When Nil tries to appear bigger than Petr and Tatiana and says that he is such a good fellow, then an aspect is lost which is so characteristic of a decent working man in Russia and that is his modesty. He boasts and quarrels, but it is clear what sort of a man he is without that. Let him be carefree, let him lark his way through all four acts, let him eat a lot after work, and that will be enough for him to conquer the audience.

Chekhov, letter to Gorky, 22 Oct. 1901,
PSS, Vol. VII (Moscow, 1970), p. 582

Nil is a man who is quietly sure of his own strength and of his right to restructure life and all its customs according to his, Nil's, own point of view. . . . He is always calm, his gestures are rounded, not abrupt, but graceful, because with each one he imparts strength, instinctively giving no more and no less than is required. . . .

Teterev wants to be a hero, but life has overwhelmed and crushed him and for that reason he hates it. He thinks he is very talented and is consequently scornful of other people. Nil is the only person whom he respects because he sees that Nil will not be mastered. . . . He hates the bourgeoisie and considers them, quite rightly, the enemies of free thinking sensitive people, and the destroyers of life. . . .

The *old man* is in an awkward situation which irritates him. He has lived a hell of a long time, worked ceaselessly, swindled to increase his profits, and suddenly sees that it has all been for nothing. . . . His children have turned out undeniably badly. And life is beginning to scare him: he no longer understands what it is about. When he speaks he cuts the air with the palm of his hand, like a knife: he raises his arm to his face and with his elbow straight, moving the hand only, he chops through the air away from his nose. His movements are slow.

Gorky, letter to Stanislavski, Jan. 1902,
SS, Vol. 28 (Moscow, 1954), p. 219

Would it not be wise for your Imperial Highness to appoint a special person to be present at the dress rehearsal of *Philistines* who could report to you on the theatrical impression made by M. Gorky's first dramatic effort? In this way we should have the opportunity of preventing public dissemination of those parts or lines which when read do not have a negative effect, but which are of the kind that in performance can provoke undesirable consequences.

V. Siniagin, Minister for Internal Affairs,
letter to Grand Duke Sergei Mikhailovich,
Governor General of Moscow, 1902, *PSS*, Vol. VII, p. 588

The whole of Petersburg government society came to the dress rehearsal at the Panaevskii Theatre where we were on tour. There were Grand Dukes and Ministers and on down through all the ranks including the whole of the censorship committee, representatives of the Police Authority, and other important people with their wives and families. A reinforced detachment of police was ordered to the theatre and the surrounding area. Cavalry were drawn up on the square in front of the theatre. You might have thought they were preparing for battle, not a dress rehearsal.

K. S. Stanislavski, 'Moia zhizn' v iskusstve',
SS, Vol. I (Moscow, 1954), p. 253-4

I often used to go and have a chat with them [students] in the interval. . . . Several performances before *Philistines* I . . . asked them not to organize any demonstrations. 'We need this play for Gorky to be able to write for the theatre. Disorder will bring a crackdown and we'll lose him.'

V. Nemirovich-Danchenko, *Iz proshlogo* (Moscow, 1936), p. 250-1

. . . and Nil, in whom the author and readers see the dawn of a new life, in fact is nothing more than another cheerful bourgeois. . . .

Iu. Aikhenval'd, *Russkaia mysl'*, Bk. II (Petersburg, 1902), p. 216,
quoted in *PSS*, Vol. VII, p. 519

Unfortunately, Petr has not found a good enough actor in Mr. Meierkhold. This is the same old intellectual with nothing to distinguish him from those this actor gives us in [Hauptmann's] and Chekhov's plays. The role of Bessemenov, the father, is a much more colourful part and is entirely successful in the hands of Mr. Luzhskii. . . . Teterev is a weapon of large calibre. The artistic roundness and clarity with which he is drawn is one of the best creations of Gorky's huge talent, and the performer of Teterev is astounding: Mr. Baranov realizes the author's intention so well and so closely identifies with the role that only Stanislavski as [Ibsen's] Dr. Stockmann can outdo him.

L. Andreev, *Kur'er*, Petersburg, 31 Mar. 1902,
Literaturnoe nasledstvo, Vol. 72 (Moscow, 1965), p. 479

The curtain falls slowly but you know that the action is not over, that it will continue, that Nil's brave speeches and challenges will not be lost. There will be a struggle and the bourgeoisie 'will go, will disappear as boils go from a healthy body'. The audience takes away not an impression of bourgeois hubbub and confusion but a greater interest in life and the knowledge that 'the future belongs to those who commit themselves to honest toil'.

I. Bibikov, *M. Gor'kii kak dramaturg* (Moscow, 1903), p. 40, quoted in *PSS*, Vol. VII, p. 595

This play . . . introduces us to the most disagreeable family we have ever seen. . . . The old father . . . spends all four acts in fits of ungovernable temper and contemptible self-pity. The mother, Akoulina, is merely a blundering old woman; the son and daughter are examples of the unhappiness of being educated above your station and capacities. . . . There are, it is true, bright spots in the picture. Nil and Polia are two of them; two more are Pertchikine . . . and Tetereff. . . . Together they bring a breath of sanity . . . which just saves the play from being wholly tedious or wholly absurd. . . . The conflict between the generations did not wait to be discovered by modern Russia. This play gives, we presume, a fair picture of the form it takes in that country. Seen by western eyes it is a dance of idiots and maniacs, and more often ridiculous than terrible. We cannot believe that it would have lost anything by being written with some regard to the laws of drama.

The Times, 24 Apr. 1906, p. 12

It was not the fault but the misfortune of previous performers and producers of *Philistines* that the Moscow Art Theatre was not successful. By marginalizing the power of the Bessemenovs of all kinds and all types the revolution has taught us to understand their characteristics as a class and to be able to recognize bourgeois behaviour in all its different forms.

S. Durylin, 'Gor'kii na stsene', *Gor'kii i teatr*, (Moscow; Leningrad, 1938), p. 237-8

When the Moscow Art Theatre returned to this play after many years in 1949, and when Stanislavski and Luzhskii's early production was resuscitated by S. K. Blinnikov and I. M. Raevskii, we saw Nil in the performance by A. Verbitskii attain sincerity, directness, and integrity. . . .

What caused the desire to rethink the interpretation of the role of Nil in the new production of *Philistines* by the BDT (Leningrad) put on in 1967? . . . The petty bourgeois frame of mind was shown in this production from within with no simplification and without turning living people into cardboard satirical representations of bourgeois types. . . [which] meant changes in the interpretation of Nil and his friends, who had to emerge the moral victors from a battle not with conventional cardboard types, but with very much more 'difficult' opponents. Here the theatre made a serious error . . . [and] began to mask those of Nil's characteristics which had led Chekhov to refer to him as heroic.

B. Bialik, *M. Gor'kii: dramaturg* (Moscow, 1977), p. 80, 83-4

Bourgeois thinking is a socially dangerous attitude . . . because people find shibboleths for themselves and believe blindly in their permanence, no longer seeing the real life beyond the fragmentary nature of their perceptions. Finding the set of delusions into which these people had fallen and which made their existence absurd was the main point of our work.

G. Tovstonogov (1967), quoted in *Istoriia russkogo sovetskogo dramaticheskogo teatra*, Vol. II (Moscow, 1987), p. 131

In Chekhov's plays the world-weariness of so many of his characters afflicts both the land-owning gentry and the intelligentsia. For Gorky, it is rooted primarily in the materialism and spiritual vacuity of the bourgeoisie and the merchant class. . . . This is worked out generationally in Gorky, for the bitter misunderstandings that exist between the Bessemenovs and their children are presented as a legacy of the past, a historic inevitability. . . . In Gorky [the revelation of psyche] is socially generalized and motivated, thereby explaining the pervasive sombreness. *The Petty Bourgeois* . . . in striking contrast to Chekhov, makes few concessions toward off-setting the overall atmosphere by anything comic or ironic. The splendid subtlety of Chekhovian nuances disappears, the middle tones wash away, and the resultant canvas is stark and emotionally overburdened.

H. Segel, *Twentieth-Century Russian Drama* (New York, 1979), p. 5-6

Fiona Shaw's Tatyana is one performance that relates the play to Gorky's mentor, Chekhov. First seen retreating from the dining table to exchange poisonous whispers with her brother, she presents a fearfully precise image of withering youth, like him sunk in helpless boredom and fear of her own feelings, and reaching a silent climax of sexual despair when she rears and collapses over the empty table like a grotesquely maimed stick insect. Performances of that quality almost reconcile you to the play.

Irving Wardle, *The Times*, 6 Apr. 1985, p. 21

It is a raw and indignant play, intermittently preachifying, bursting with talent, short on subtlety, and full of that combination of brutality and sentimentality which characterizes so much of Gorky's work. Strindberg is the only other dramatist I know who could so intensely dislike his own characters as well as profoundly understand them. The exception is Nil. . . . Gorky is at his worst with this kind of dewy-eyed writing. He must have known perfectly well that such messiahs of brave new worlds are usually humourless, egocentric, life-hating, and ruthless; it is such lies of the imagination as this that lay the foundations for socialist realism and all its intolerant evils.

John Peter, *Sunday Times*, 7 Apr. 1985, p. 43

Tom Mannion has chosen to display Nil's working-class credentials by speaking the part with a Scottish accent, and during his more fatuous outbursts ('I'll make life give me the answers I want!') the listener falls to wondering when and how he made the difficult childhood journey from Glasgow. . . .

Julian Graffy, *Times Literary Supplement*,
3 May 1985, p. 497

The Lower Depths

'Pictures. Four Acts.'
Written: 1902. Awarded Griboedov Prize, 1904.
First production: MAT, 18 Dec. 1902 (dir. K. S. Stanislavski and
V. I. Nemirovich-Danchenko; des. V. A. Simov; with Stanislavski
as Satin, O. Knipper as Nastia, I. M. Moskvin as Luka, V. V. Luzhskii
as Bubnov, and M. F. Andreeva as Natasha).
Major revivals: no permission granted for imperial theatres by censor
without extensive cuts, but provincial performances at Viatsk, Kiev,
Nizhegorod, Rostov on the Don, Tiflis, Kherson, Krasnoiarsk,
1903-05; Orenburg, 1904; Ekaterinburg, 1906, 1910, 1914;
Kostroma, 1906, 1908; Gadiach, 1908; Voronezh, 1908;
Tiflis, 1908; Ekaterinodar, Khar'kov, 1910; Kazan', 1912;
Nizhegorod, 1915.

17

Major revivals of the Soviet period: Gosdrama Th., Petrograd
(afterwards Pushkin Th. of Drama), 1919, to celebrate Gorky's
fiftieth birthday; among numerous revivals at a large number of other
theatres, by the sixtieth anniversary of the premiere (1962) there had
been 1,451 performances at MAT; Sovremennik Theatre, Moscow,
1968 (dir. G. Volchek; des. P. Kirillov; with I. Kvasha as Luka, and
E. Evstigneev as Satin).

First production abroad: Kleines Th., Berlin, 23 Jan. 1903
(dir. Max Reinhardt and Richard Vallentin; with Reinhardt as Luka
and Vallentin as Satin).

Revived: Volksbühne, Berlin, 1926 (dir. Erwin Piscator).

First London production: Stage Society, Court Th., trans. Great Queen
Street Th., 23 Nov. 1903. (dir. Max Behrend).

Revived: Great Queen Street Th., 16 Feb 1906 (German Company);
Kingsway Th., 2 Dec 1911 (dir. John Pollock and Frank Collins);
MAT (Prague Group) tour, Garrick Th., 13 Apr. 1928; RSC,
New Arts Th. Club, 9 May 1962 (dir. Toby Robertson;
des. Hutchinson Scott); RSC, Aldwych Th., 29 June 1972
(dir. David Jones; des. Timothy O'Brien; with Gordon Gostelow
as Luka and Bernard Lloyd as Satin).

First American production: Plymouth Th., New York, 22 Dec. 1919
(dir. Arthur Hopkins; with Edward G. Robinson as Satin and Pauline
Lord as Nastia).

Revived: MAT tour, 59th Street Th., New York, Jan. 1923.

Films: Bas-Fonds, 1936 (dir. Jean Renoir); Donzoko, 1957
(dir. Akira Kurosawa).

First published: as *Na dne zhizni*, Munich, 1903; as *Na dne*, St.
Petersburg: 'Znanie', 1903.

Translations: as *In the Depths*, in Alfred Bates, *The Drama: Its History,
Literature, and Influence on Civilization* (London, 1903); as *Night's
Lodging*, tr. E. Hopkins (Boston: Badger, 1905), reissued as
Submerged: Scenes from Russian Life in Four Acts, 1915;
tr. L. Irving (London: Unwin; New York: Duffield, 1912); as
The Dregs of Humanity, in *The Warner Library: the World's Best
Literature* (New York, 1917), and in *The Columbia Course in
Literature, Vol. 1* (New York, 1928); tr. J. Covan (New York,
Brentano, 1922), and in Oliver Sayler, *The Moscow Art Theatre
Series of Plays* (New York, 1923); in Samuel M. Tucker, *Modern
Continental Plays* (New York, 1929); as *At the Bottom*, tr.
W. Laurence (New York: French, 1930); as *Down and Out*,
tr. G. Noyes and A. Kaun, in G. R. Noyes, *Masterpieces of Russian
Drama* (New York; London, 1933); in R. B. Mantle and J. Gassner,
A Treasury of Theatre (New York, 1935); in Thomas H. Dickinson,
Continental Plays (Boston, 1935); in Charles H. Whitman,

Representative Modern Dramas (New York: Macmillan, 1936); in Harlan H. Hatcher, *Modern Continental Dramas* (New York, 1941); in Bennett Cerf and Van H. Cartmell, *Sixteen European Plays* (New York, 1943); as *The Lowest Depths*, in B. G. Guerney, *A Treasury of Russian Literature* (New York, 1943; London, 1948); tr. M. Wettlin, in *Five Plays* (Moscow, 1956), and in *Collected Works in Ten Volumes, Vol. IV* (Moscow 1978-80); tr. A. Bakshy and Paul Nathan, in *Seven Plays* (New Haven; London, 1946); tr. A. Bakshy and Paul S. Nathan, in *The Lower Depths and Other Plays* (New Haven, 1959); in David Magarshack, *The Storm and other Russian Plays* (New York, 1960); tr. Kitty Hunter-Blair and Jeremy Brooks (London: Methuen, 1973).
Adaptation: by Tunde Ikoli, 1986.

Destitute murderers, alcoholics, thieves, vagrants, and other casualties of life rent space in a gloomy cellar doss-house in Moscow at the turn of the century. Kostylev, the drunken and violent owner, his wife Vasilisa, and her sister Natasha live above. Luka, a vagrant with religious pretensions, makes it his business to offer comfort to the troubled and sick, and controverts the hard philosophy of doss-house life by offering Anna, dying of consumption, hope of heaven; by promising the alcoholic Actor a cure; and by encouraging others to believe in their dreams in the face of the rank impossibility of achieving them. A 'domestic' drama is also unfolding: a young thief Pepel is caught between the affections of Vasilisa and Natasha. Vasilisa finally suggests that if Pepel cares to arrange her husband's death she will set up his escape with Natasha. Their conversation is overheard by Luka, who tries to persuade Pepel to make his escape immediately. Luka has stimulated a debate among the dossers on the merits of truth and lies in their survival of life's injustices, but disappears during the brawl in Act 3 in which Kostylev is killed by Pepel. Pepel and Vasilisa are arrested and Natasha disappears. The Actor is distraught because Luka failed to give him the details of where to go for his cure. Satin, a murderer and thief, takes up the debate in Act 4, and defends the dignity of all human beings whatever their station: their dignity makes them worthy of the truth, although he also understands Luka's need to offer comfort and humanity's need to receive it. The Actor's suicide at the close of the play offers a pointed comment on the consequences of Luka's attitude.

I want to bring the sun to the stage, a joyful little sun, a Russian one — not very bright, but caressing and embracing everything. If only I were able!

> Gorky, letter to K. S. Stanislavski, late 1900,
> *SS*, Vol. 28 (Moscow, 1954), p. 147-8

Act 2 is very good. It's the best and most powerful, and when I read it, especially the ending, I nearly leapt with pleasure. The mood is gloomy and heavy, and the audience will walk out of the theatre because they are not accustomed to this, and you can say farewell to your reputation as an optimist. . . . [Act 4)] could appear boring and superfluous, especially after the stronger and more interesting characters have departed, and only the run-of-the-mill are left. The death of the actor is horrible. You really are boxing the spectators' ears without having prepared them. . . . Don't hurry with the title. You'll think of something.

> Chekhov, letter to Gorky, 29 July 1902,
> in *M. Gor'kii i A. Chekhov: perepiska. stat' i i vyskazyvaniia*
> (Moscow, 1951)

The title is everything. Do you understand? You have to hit the audience right between the eyes. Someone wrote a play. He showed it to me. I read 'At the Bottom of Life'. It's stupid! Flat. Just write 'At the Bottom'. That's all. Do you understand? I saved the person. The title is a subtle thing.

> Leonid Andreev, as quoted by I. A. Bunin,
> 'Avtobiograficheskie zametki', *Sob. soch..*, Vol. 1
> (Berlin, 1936), p. 61-2

Gorky's new play can only be given permission for performance if very significant excisions and changes are made. It goes without saying that the policeman Medvedev must be changed into an ordinary retired soldier, since the involvement of a policeman with rank in many of the escapades of the night shelter's inhabitants is not permissible on the stage. The end of the second act should be shortened considerably. In deference to the death of Kleshch's consumptive wife, the coarse conversations which take place after her demise should be omitted. The pilgrim's speeches need cutting: there are many statements about God, future life, falsehood, and other subjects. Finally, individual sentences and the rough and coarse expressions need cutting throughout the play.

> S. Trubachev (censor's report), Aug. 1902,
> quoted in *PSS*, Vol. VII, p. 606

I had the impression that the play was only finally passed because the authorities were certain of its complete failure in performance. . . .

> V. Nemirovich-Danchenko, letter to B. Kachalov,
> quoted in *PSS*, Vol. VII, p. 610

[For *The Lower Depths*] we have had to evolve a tone which is new for our theatre. A light, quick, and strong one which doesn't cram the play with unnecessary pauses and details of little interest. This has placed more responsibility on the actors. . . .

> V. Nemirovich-Danchenko, letter to Chekhov, 13 Dec. 1902,
> *Teatral'noe nasledie*, Vol. 1 (Moscow, 1952), p. 112

Gorky has turned sharply towards cheerfulness and raising people's spirits. His new play is startling in its force, its boldness, and its beauty.

> Leonid Andreev, letter to N. K. Mikhailovskii, Aug. 1902,
> *Literaturnoe nasledstvo*, Vol. 72 (Moscow, 1965), p. 495

At the end of the play the length of the ovation was unprecedented. Gorky was called out more than fifteen times. . . . Words cannot describe what happened when Gorky finally appeared alone. We cannot recall a dramatist enjoying such success.

> *Russkoe slovo*, 19 Dec. 1902, quoted in *PSS*, Vol. VII, p. 613

Nowhere except in this amazing theatre would this play have been a success. Vladimir Ivanovich Danchenko has interpreted the play so well, and has worked at it so that not one word is lost. The acting is staggering. . . . I only saw and understood at the first performance the astounding leap that all these people have made. They are used to acting Ibsen's and Chekhov's characters. What a denial of themselves. The second performance was even more striking for the harmony of the whole thing. The audience roars and laughs. Just think, in spite of the number of dead in the play, there is laughter in the theatre through all four acts.

> Gorky, letter to K. P. Piatnitskii, 20 or 21 Dec. 1902,
> *SS*, Vol. 28 (Moscow, 1954), p. 277

Gorky's magnificent concept is so outrageously and daringly accomplished by the actors that you catch your breath. . . . Luka is a peasant, a wanderer, a holy fool, a joker who brings a purely Russian note into the action. . . . The baron . . . he's just magnificent. He's such a bastard, a naive bastard! . . . The theatre is no longer theatre, but life, where there are no actors, there are people — good and bad, but no longer actors.

M. V. Nesterov, 1902,
quoted in PSS, Vol. VII, p. 615

Neither the audiences, nor the critics have got to the heart of the play. They go on praising but they don't want to understand. I try to understand who is to blame. Moskvin's talent as Luka or the lack of skill of the author. I am not very happy.

Gorky, letter to K. P. Piatnitskii, 7 Jan. 1903,
SS, Vol. 28 (Moscow, 1954), p. 279

In April I went to performances of two plays by Stanislavski's troupe: Chekhov's *Uncle Vanya* and Gorky's *Lower Depths*. Listening to the many comments about these plays, I came to the conclusion that as much as the audiences understood the first play, so they misunderstood the second. The Petersburg theatregoing public is as far from the inhabitants of the night-shelter as an inhabitant of New Zealand is from us. And of course the audiences criticize the play, finding it coarse, cynical, unlifelike, and so on. . . . If the thousands of people sitting in the boxes in their brilliant evening wear just knew how much lower their own morality is than that of Luka, Satin, Vas'ka, Pepel, and Natasha. In their souls seeds will never ripen, however much they are watered by the words of Luka and others like him. These people have decayed along with their books, their clever thoughts, and their ostentatious morality.

A. N. Tolstoi, 'O p'ese M. Gor'kogo Na dne', 1903,
Sob. soch., Vol. 10 (Moscow, 1961), p. 7-9

[Gorky:] In [*The Lower Depths*] there is no opposition to what Luka says. The main question I wanted to pose is which is better: truth or pity? Which is the more necessary? Should pity be taken to the point where you're actually lying like Luka? This isn't a subjective question but a general philosophical issue. Luka is the incarnation of compassion, and even of the lie as a means of salvation. . . .

[Correspondent:] From our conversation with Mr. Gorky we have concluded that in spite of what the critics have written, the sympathies of the author of *The Lower Depths* are not on the side of those who profess the necessity of lies and pity. On the contrary, he is on the side of those striving for truth. However bitter and sad the truth may be, it is more necessary and better than the beautiful lie.

L. Nemanov, *Peterburgskaia gazeta*, 15 June 1903, quoted in *PSS*, Vol. VII, p. 617

Satin's words about man being the truth mean something entirely different, but by some strange confusion of ideas the author and the majority of the critics believe that Satin, in uttering these words, is somehow explicating the old man's crafty teaching. . . . Luka does not forget immediate, physical humanity: he cares for mankind solicitously. Because he respects him, because he values his human worth, Luka deceives man; such is the bitter irony of his actions as opposed to his words. Respect out of pity! 'You've got to respect man! Not pity him, not demean him by pity, but respect him,' says Satin, explaining the meaning of Luka's teaching. Yet one cannot help but feel that he is mocking him.

A. Volshski, *Zhurnal dlia vsekh*, No. 11-12, (St. Petersburg, 1904), tr. Stanley Rabinowitz, in *The Noise of Change* (Ann Arbor, 1986), p. 72-3

This drama of Gorky's apparently seeks to avoid every stage convention, and succeeds. . . .

The Times, 17 Feb. 1906, p. 16

Previously Fate has picked royal victims. . . . Now Fate has perceived that the game is not without a certain pleasure with less rare individuals, and that she can be satisfied with a Kleshch or a Satin. These days even the most ordinary setting is not disdained; moreover once the romantic effects and the world of superhuman passions are abandoned, knowledge of psychopathology and crime statistics can be put to excellent use.

I. F. Annenskii, 'Drama na dne', *Kniga otrazhenii* (St. Petersburg, 1906; Moscow, 1979), p. 71

We consider Gorky's clear sympathy with Luka a temporary lapse in a writer who is dear to us and in whose campaigning instinct we believe.

A. Lunacharskii, 1906, *Sob. soch.*, Vol. 2 (Moscow, 1964), p. 11

The last word in the macabre. It turns the theatre into a chamber of horrors . . . harrowing . . . the undercurrent of listless despair, the numbing sense of there being no way out.

The Times, 4 Dec. 1911, p. 6

23

Slum society all the world over, one feels, must be much like that of Kostylov's underground shelter.

The Athenaeum, 9 Dec. 1911

With a firm sense of the dramatic and little sense of the theatre, he has in *The Lower Depths* aimed to interest us in his characters, to revolt us against their degradation. He is the apostle of the poor. . . . They stand stark and naked to the eye. That Russian desire to penetrate into the absolute, to probe the depths and mysteries of life, is apparent in the exile's dramas. We are very near to earth, yet we are constantly searching for heaven.

L. H. W., review of translation by L. Irving,
New York Review of Books, 1 Sept. 1912

The theatre has never once been as full as today. We had to shut the box office and hide from the public. People stood in the aisles, in the boxes, in every corner. The police arrived in the interval, demanding that there should be some order. Newspaper correspondents besieged us. . . .

K. S. Stanislavski, on MAT tour in Berlin, 8 Oct. 1922,
Sob. soch. (Moscow, 1959), p. 401

Gorky told me that Moskvin took Luka too seriously. Luka is in reality a cunning man. He has been trampled on so he is soft, as he says of himself. Luka knows how to apply a plaster of lies to every wound.

A. Lunacharskii, *Literaturnye siluety*
(Moscow; Leningrad, 1925), p. 142

You ask why in *The Lower Depths* there is no call to rebellion? You can hear this call in Satin's words containing his evaluation of man. Why did I take such 'ex'-people and why make them say what they do in the play? Because these people have become detached from their class and are free of bourgeois prejudice. They have nothing to lose, but in this lies all their good.

Gorky, letter to Red Army soldiers, 1928,
SS, Vol. 24 (Moscow, 1953), p. 357-8

Laughter in this terrible play of Maxim Gorki's . . . is an encounter full of surprise and illumination. True, it is not the easy laughter of entertainment; it does not arise, in all conscience, from frivolity of mind or from lightness of heart. . . . It is desperate, but it has merriment in it. It is sometimes infinitely sad, but it is as often childlike. It is a voice of misery and disillusionment; it is a bragging in the face of circumstance; it can be harsh, can be cruel, can be a cry against nature herself — but, from cruelty and grief, pity marvellously springs, and is to be heard in the voices of these men and women who laugh because they suffer, and suffer because they must.

The Times, 14 Apr. 1928, p. 8

From everything I have said about this play, I hope it is clear how unsuccessful it was . . . an outmoded play, and perhaps even harmful in our day. Although this self-criticism is late, I have to say that it was generated not now, in 1932, but before the revolution. I do not consider it without use for those young comrades who process the content of their observations too hastily and carelessly. In our times the comforter can be shown on the stage only as a negative or comic figure.

Gorky, 'O p'esakh', *God 16-tyi, Al'manakh 1* (Moscow, 1933)

Sombre and uncompromising with a certain midnight beauty, it was something wider audiences should have shared. One player towered: Wilfrid Lawson as Luka, the wanderer, who is gentle because he has been through the mill so often. Stiff, stocky, his slow voice convulsively exact, he dominated the night by force of imagination.

Wendy and J. C. Trewin, on RSC production of 1962,
The Arts Theatre, London, 1927-1981 (London, 1986), p. 66

The reasons for the long delayed impact of Gorky on the English theatre are complex. . . . They relate to the fact that the explosion of talent in 1956 was politically of the Left, whereas the commercial theatre had been overwhelmingly of the Right as its neglect of Gorky . . . confirms.

Laurence Kitchin, *Drama in the Sixties*
(London, 1966), p. 101.

The famous monologue about man was not delivered [by Evstigneev] with pathos or the usual rhetoric, but as a tragic confession. It is tragic to think about the destiny of humanity in the dark hole of the cellar dosshouse. Evstigneev spoke quietly, without emotion or bitterness, with tears in his eyes; the long familiar words were a revelation.

T. K. Shakh-Azizova,
Istoriia russkogo sovetskogo dramaticheskogo teatra,
Vol. 2 (Moscow, 1987), p. 133

Gorky's thieves, card-sharps, and fallen nobility are not Embankment dossers or meths drinkers. Whatever their claims to universality they are first of all intensely Russian. And to that extent any foreign company is working in a vacuum inventing temperamental resources to fill up these stormy, violent abstractions, and thus denying the realistic premises of the play. . . . What gets through strongly, if spasmodically, in this production is the mutual torment the situation drives them to. As they cannot punish their real (and unnamed) oppressors, they punish each other, or they punish themselves.

Irving Wardle, *The Times*, 30 June 1972

There is enormous disagreement about where Gorky stood philosophically. The Marxists have muddied the waters beyond belief since his death (probably murdered by Stalin's order). There are some who find his jokes, his laughter, his songs amid the bleakest of misery sentimental. I don't. I feel that Gorky was there and that was how life was in the lower depths. . . . Gordon Gostelow I thought a marvellous Luka (it's a dream of a role). . . . David Jones's direction was marvellously coherent — for which I am grateful — but I felt the highs and the lows were a little close, that there wasn't enough variation in mood.

John Crosby, *Plays and Players*,
Vol. 19, No. 11 (Aug. 1972), p. 47

Russian acting is very extravagant. . . . [There's] a temperamental difference, and that's what they'd got to try and achieve as English actors — an ability to move quickly and in extremes from a tragic mood into a comic mood, or to be absolutely vicious to somebody one moment and terribly sweet the next. It's a sort of volatility of temperament which is not English. . . .

David Jones, 'Directing Gorky',
Theatre Quarterly, Vol. 3, No. 9 (1973), p. 14

On the basis of *The Petty Bourgeois* and other earlier (and later) works, the case may be argued rather convincingly that Gorky rejects the palliatives freely dispensed by Luka. Textually, however, Luka is presented as operating from essentially virtuous motives, so the character must not be regarded as entirely negative. Then, the later suicide of Actor and the lack of impact of Satin's passionate monologues on the subject of truth and man . . . indicate . . . a certain ambivalence on Gorky's part.

Harold B. Segel, *Twentieth-Century Russian Drama*
(New York, 1979), p. 10

The glorification of Man brought a particular strength to a work which pointed an accusing finger at the whole of the old world.

B. Bialik, *M. Gor'kii: dramaturg* (Moscow, 1977), p. 153

Gorky seems to agree with Luka that man, in order to grow as a human being, needs to have something to believe in. This belief is a kind of catalyst that brings forth the best in man: strength, resistance, love. . . . The conviction of the necessity of belief later brought Gorky to the philosophy of 'god-building': if God does not exist, man must create him himself, for moral reasons. However, Gorky's ambivalence in *The Lower Depths* lies in the treatment of this belief as an illusion. The writer . . . turns Luka's belief into a 'life-line' that helped the individual being in his existential situation, without helping him out of it.

Geir Kjetsaa, 'Ambivalence in Attitude: the Character of Luka in *The Lower Depths*', *Russian Literature*, XXIV (Amsterdam, 1988), p. 519-20

The Lower Depths . . . in its rags, remained strikingly current through time, translations, and performances. His other plays did not have that demonic robustness. They all had an air of militant political sermonizing about them. . . . He believed in his mission as an educator even if it should be a little detrimental to the artistic quality of his work.

Henri Troyat, *Gorky* (London, 1991), p. 181-2

Summerfolk

'Scenes.' A play in four acts.
Written: 1904.
First production: V. F. Komissarzhevskaia's Th., St. Petersburg, 10 Nov. 1904 (dir. I. A. Tikhomirov; with Komissarzhevskaia as Varvara).
Revived: K. N. Nezlobin's Th., Riga, 30 Nov. 1904 (dir. K. A. Mardzhanov); Nizhegorod Th., 1904; at many provincial theatres, including Rostov on the Don, Ekaterinburg, Saratov (dir. N. I. Sobolschikov-Samarin), 1905.
Major revivals of the Soviet period : BDT, Leningrad, 1939 (dir. B. A. Babochkin; des. A. F. Bosulaev); Ermolova Th., Moscow, 1949 (dir. A. M. Lobanov); MAT, 1953 (dir. M. N. Kedrov and V. Orlov); Malyi Th., Moscow, 1964 (dir. B. Babochkin; des. A. Bosulaev; with Babochkin as Suslov); BDT, Leningrad, 1976 (dir. G. Tovstonogov; des. E. Kochergin).

First British production: RSC, Aldwych Th., 27 Aug.1974 (tr. Kitty Hunter-Blair and Jeremy Brooks; dir. David Jones; des. Timothy O'Brien and Tazeena Firth; with Norman Rodway as Basov, Susan Fleetwood as Kaleriia, Mike Gwilym as Vlas), toured to Brooklyn Academy of Music, New York, 5 Feb. 1975.

Revived: Schaubuhne am Halleschen Ufer at Lyttelton Th., London, 3 Mar. 1977 (adapted by Peter Stein and Botho Strauss); Chichester Festival Th., 22 May 1989 (tr. Michael Robinson; dir. Sam Mendes; des. Paul Farnsworth; with Peter McEnery as Shalimov and Kate Duchene as Kaleriia).

First published: Sbornik 'Znanie' za 1904g, Bk. III, St. Petersburg, 1905.

Translations: as *Summer Folk*, Boston, 1905; tr. A. Delano, in *Poet Lore*, XVI, No. 3 (1905); tr. M. Wettlin, in *Five Plays* (Moscow, 1956), and in *Collected Works in Ten Volumes, Vol. 4* (Moscow, 1978-80); tr. Kitty Hunter-Blair and Jeremy Brooks, in Gorky, *Five Plays* (London: Methuen, 1988).

Chalets sited in the forest and let to summer visitors provide the setting for a close look at the educated professional class in Russia at the turn of the century. Ironically framed by the preparations of a group of amateur thespians, the action focuses on the Basovs, who have invited a famous writer, Shalimov, to stay. His banality precipitates divisions within this social group. Various love affairs and business scandals are revealed, while a sincere relationship between a middle-aged lady doctor, Maria Lvovna, and Vlas, a young lawyer in his twenties, is vilified by their peers. Stung into reaction, Maria Lvovna claims that they as a group are wasting their energy and leisure on discussion and on artistic pursuits when, as the vanguard of the professional class, they should be working for social change and defending the interests of the deprived. As the relationships come under strain, Varvara, too, finally acknowledges the mundanity of her husband, rejects a lover who attempts suicide, and walks out on her marriage and family in search of a more purposeful life.

Summerfolk leaves the listener unmoved for all four hours of its reading . . . and it holds the attention in four or five places only. . . . Lack of clarity of the author's own beliefs . . . he is inclined to negate or is inclined to love what he is attacking with indignation . . . ordinariness

and flatness of his methods . . . the question of how Mar'ia L'vovna will
deal with the feelings overwhelming her — to fight or to yield — on this
issue the author is not writing as a great poet, to whose words practically
the whole world is listening at the moment.

> V. Nemirovich-Danchenko, review of Gorky's script,
> 1904, *PSS*, Vol. VII, p. 634

Having carefully read your review of my play, I felt from your attitude
to questions which I have already firmly and irrevocably decided that
there is a major difference of opinion between us. This difference is
insurmountable, and so I find it impossible to give my play to a theatre
run by you.

> Gorky, letter to V. Nemirovich-Danchenko, 1904,
> *PSS*, Vol. VII, p. 634

I have never felt and will probably never feel again my own power and
my meaning in life to such a degree and so deeply as at that moment
after the third act when I stood right by the footlights, completely carried
away by a wild pleasure, not bowing my head before the audience, but
ready for anything — if only someone would hiss at me. . . .

> Gorky, letter to E. P. Peshkova, 25 or 26 Nov. 1904,
> *SS*, Vol. 28 (Moscow, 1954), p. 333

During my long years of sitting in theatres I have never had the occasion
to observe such changes of mood in the audience . . . and such a split in
the audience in general.

> A. P. Kugel, *Rus*, 11 Nov. 1904,
> quoted in *PSS*, Vol. VII, p. 640

I found the play extremely boring, overlong, and in any case much
weaker than all of Gorky's previous plays. . . . Add to that the whistling
and the fact that the author was still affected by Stanislavskii's refusal to
accept the play, and you can understand his nasty state of mind during
the performance.

> D. Merezhkovskii, interviewed in *Peterburgskaia gazeta*,
> 12 Nov. 1904, quoted in *PSS*, Vol. VII, p. 641

The second act engaged the audience immediately with its unusual and
original set. Chalets with verandahs and fences, flowerbeds, benches,

hedges, and a stage for the amateur performance were literally piled on top of one another. The actors had to keep to one spot which created an impression of senseless hustle and bustle. Gorky was pleased that 'everyone had to gather around Basov's chalet. . . . The Russian intelligentsia has just such a small stage of action in real life.'

V. P. Gardin, *Vospominaniia*, Vol. 2 (Moscow, 1952), p. 183, quoted in E. Dubnova, 'M.Gor'kii i teatr V. F. Komissarzhevskoi', *Gor'kovskie chteniia* (Moscow, 1968), p. 161

The more beautiful the surrounding Shishkin-like forest seemed, the more ghastly became all this society of summerfolk, among whom everything was the same: the fences all painted red, identical little verandahs hung round with canvas blinds . . . all the same with no regard to different fashions, a greyness of thought, of feelings, and of mood.

A. P. Kugel', *Teatr i iskusstvo*, No. 46 (1904), p. 812, quoted in E. Dubnova, 'M. Gor'kii i teatr V. F. Komissarzhevskoi', *Gor'kovskie chteniia* (Moscow, 1968), p. 161

After the third act, in which the daughter approves her mother's taking of a lover, the stalls began to hiss, and the gallery began to call for the author more than before. At first he didn't come, then he came out and stood near the footlights. He stared, not bowing to the audience and looked at them with scorn. I expected him to stick his tongue out at us. But the audience was overjoyed and clapped furiously. And the actors led by Komissarzhevskaia also clapped.

S. I. Smirnova-Sazonova, quoted in E. Dubnova, as above, p. 163

While Gorky protests and negates . . . it is impossible not to sympathise with him . . . but as soon as Gorky goes over to assertion, then his talent betrays him; his thoughts are confused and something impossibly coarse and philistine emerges. . . . Mar'ia L'vovna, Basova [Varvara], and Vlas prove to the dead they are dead. . . . They leave in triumph, supported by the capitalist, and celebrate a cheap victory with the applauding audience. . . . Surely it is clear that these petty, pitiable people, abandoning the old banality, must inevitably find a new one: only that person can avoid the new banality who arrives not spiritually impoverished but with reserves of cultural values brought from the past.

D. Filsofov, 'Zavtrashnee meshchanstvo', *Novyi put'*, Nov. 1904, quoted in *PSS*, Vol. VII, p. 642

Here [in Riga] *Summerfolk* is much better, M. F. Andreeva is very good
as Mar'ia L'vovna. . . .

> Gorky, letter to K. P. Piatnitskii, 4 Dec. 1904,
> quoted in *PSS*, Vol. VII, p. 644

This is the intelligentsia, not the old aristocratic intelligentsia, but a
bourgeois one. These are the Petr Bessemenevs of different hues and
different ages; the Tatianas and Shishkins. All of them have risen by
means of education above the level of the petty bourgeoisie and seek a
firm place in our changing Russian society. . . .

As far as the positive characters are concerned . . . their refreshing
good spirits, their simplicity, the sincerity of their relationships, the
poetry of their directness and self-confidence are well caught. These
characteristics are typical of the best individuals from the proletarian
intelligentsia. All the same, in comparison with the richly drawn negative
characters, these positive types seem impressionistically sketched-in
outlines. . . .

As a work of art, as a faithfully conceived and splendidly executed
general picture which reflects the inner life of a whole layer of our
society, Gorky's new play is a major, gratifying literary event.

> A. Lunacharskii, 'Dachniki', *Pravda*, St. Petersburg, Apr. 1905,
> in *Sob. soch.*, Vol. 2 (Moscow, 1964), p. 11, 28, 29

The production was not a clear-cut, black and white one: people against
people or the pure and free versus the predatory and pathetic. A
magnificent, calm backdrop from nature stood against the over-fussy
'summerfolk'. The sheer breadth, endlessness, and calm of the Russian
landscape [des. A. Bosulaev] brought a lyric, poetic atmosphere to contrast with the trivial existence of the 'summerfolk'.

> T. K. Shakh-Azizova,
> *Istoriia russkogo sovetskogo dramaticheskogo teatra*,
> Vol. II (Moscow, 1987), p. 131

I can't help wondering if Chekhov's lonely pre-eminence amongst
Russian dramatists isn't long overdue for reassessment. Gorky lacks
Chekhov's sheer mastery of symphonic structure. . . . But his plays cover
a much wider social spectrum, have a comparable richness of texture,
and return again and again to the paramount theme of twentieth-century
drama: how much truth can human beings actually stand? . . . I can see
the problems any director faces: keeping in sharp focus a multiplicity of
characters . . . and capturing that volatility of mood that is the keynote of

Russian drama . . . the emotional fullness demanded by this rich, yeasty, madly neglected, and damnably difficult play.

Michael Billington, *The Guardian*, 27 Aug. 1974, p. 10

The difference [from Chekhov] lies in Gorky's positive commitment to social action. . . . What I find most fascinating however is the play's timelessness: the Russian intelligentsia of 1904 as portrayed by Gorky is, ironically, in the same position as the Russian intelligentsia of today. They too are largely people who have risen by their own exertions at universities, polytechnics, or in party work; they too are anxious to enjoy their new-found status, and they too, like Shalimov, the writer, or Bassov, the lawyer, or Kaleria, the bluestocking, therefore prefer not to look at reality, to dismiss any thought of working for the oppressed and underprivileged. . . . Today's Vlasses and Maria Lvovnas on the other hand are the Sakharovs and Solzhenitsyns who cry in the wilderness urging their fellow intellectuals to open their eyes and to take action against the Byzantine establishment of their society.

David Jones has produced this brilliant and thought-provoking play with a firm grasp of its outline and its teeming detail. The acting is uniformly good: I should like to single out Susan Fleetwood who, discarding the easy advantages of her youth and beauty, brilliantly characterizes an aging, hysterical old maid and bluestocking: the over-intensity born of frustration with which she twists and turns, the false, self-deprecating modesty which is merely another aspect of her insane arrogance, these are not only observed with amazing clinical accuracy, they are also truly tragic. Mike Gwilym also gives a noteworthy performance: he makes the Oedipal erotic infatuation of a young boy for an older woman — a mother figure — deeply credible, and also manages the sardonic humour of the clown with despair in his heart with great wit and incisiveness of attack.

Martin Esslin, *Plays and Players*, Oct. 1974, p. 29

There is an element lacking in English audiences which is not lacking on the continent. It's the experience of having been invaded and occupied by an alien power. Nor have we experienced revolution when what you say today might have the consequence of whether you live or die tomorrow. For this reason we've failed to connect with those European dramas in which the dialectic of politics is a matter of life and death. Plays like *Tango* or *The Plebeians Rehearse the Uprising* don't really hit English audiences in their guts. For some reason, works like *Summerfolk* and *Enemies* do. . . . We may not have experienced invasion or revolution but we can still understand the threat of disruption from within — people dividing against themselves. It's just beginning to matter in this country what other people are saying and thinking, where one stands politically. That's the position of Gorky's middle class yesterday. It's not so far removed from the problems of our society today.

Jeremy Brooks, quoted by Peter Ansorge,
Plays and Players, Oct. 1974, p. 14

Summerfolk is sometimes produced as a satire on the bourgeois degeneration of Chekhov's characters. Tovstonogov's production sounded a different note: the majority of his characters had never been Chekhovian characters. They were either too petty or too aggressive for that. The setting still retained the form, poetic spirit, and ambience of Chekhov: green curtains floating from the rig seemed to absorb all the green of spring, and the glow of nature's colours (des. E. Kochergin). But this was no longer the world of 'summerfolk'. . . . Not one scrap of spirituality was glimpsed in these people, living their ragged, thoughtless, banal, noisy lives as if in a badly directed amateur production. Basov's banal fussiness and Suslov's almost biological malice were seen through the eyes of the one Chekhovian character. It was as if one of the three sisters had somehow accidentally turned up in 'summerfolk' society. Varavara Basova [L. Malevannaia] was incompatible with these people . . . defenceless but determined.

V. A. Maksimova,
Istoriia russkogo-sovetskogo dramaticheskogo teatra, Vol. II
(Moscow, 1987), p. 189

Herr Stein's transfixing production which marries soft naturalism (I have not heard incidental stage sounds — the jangle of glasses, the rattle of dice — so carefully conveyed since the ring of the axe in the Moscow Art Theatre's *Cherry Orchard*) to hard symbolism (in the way a scene will freeze in one part of the stage as the emphasis switches to another). The result is that Gorky's game of Unhappy Families becomes far more than is contained in the frustrations and agonies of these characters.

Sunday Times, 6 Mar. 1977, p. 37

The main development, the growing awareness of Vlas and Varvara, has nothing to do with the play's various unfolding love affairs. Love, in fact, motivates Varvara and Vlas by its negative impact. . . . Love to Gorky's summer folk is a summer pastime, not an existential problem — even Ryumin, the romantic suicide, fails in his act of despair. . . .

The play presumes a sense of action, but no unity of action: the stage is full of activities — singing, courting, arguing. Each activity is short; it builds up neither a story nor a coherent plot, but merely an occasional illusion of an affair and an atmosphere of boredom and discontent, summed up periodically by one person, Varvara. The only axis of the play . . . is the process of the protagonist's transformation.

> Yael Harussi, 'Realism in Drama: Turgenev, Chekhov, Gorky, and their Summer Folk', *Ulbandus Review*, Vol. 2, Part 2 (1982), p. 139-41

Gorky's play was produced in the same year as Chekhov's *Cherry Orchard* but already we are in a changed world. It is as though the creaking cherry trees have been chopped down and replaced with dachas where townees can come and take the country air. . . . Sam Mendes . . . uses a version of the text that has swapped scenes, cut characters, altered entrances, all in the interest of clarity. The surgery is bold, the result superb.

> Jeremy Kingston, *The Times*, 23 May 1989, p. 20

One large reservation. Why commission a new translation of a Russian play from a German version by Botho Stauss and Peter Stein when there's a fine one available, translated from the Russian, by Jeremy Brooks? . . . This is not just a case of Buy British. The Strauss-Stein version alters the play's structure, switches around some of Gorky's dialogue, and invents bits he never wrote.

> John Peter, *Sunday Times*, 28 May 1989, p. 9

Children of the Sun

A play in four acts.
Written: 1905.
First productions: Komissarzhevskaia's Th., Petersburg, 12 Oct. 1905 (dir. N. N. Arbatov; with V. F. Komissarzhevskaia as Liza and K. V. Bravich as Protasov); MAT, 24 Oct. 1905 (dir. K. S. Stanislavski and V. Nemirovich-Danchenko; with V. I. Kachalov as Protasov, M. F. Andreeva as Liza, O. Knipper as Melaniia, and N. M. Moskvin as Nazar).
Major Soviet revivals: Kamernyi Th., Moscow, 1935 (dir. A. Tairov); Russian Th., Kiev, 1936 (dir. B. Nord; des. L. Al'shitz; with M. Romanov as Protasov); Ermolova Th., Moscow, 1937

(dir. N. P. Khmelev); Iaroslavl' Dramatic Th., 1962 (dir. F. Shishigin;
des. A. Ippolitov); Vakhtangov Th., Moscow, Oct. 1968
(dir. E. Simenev and E. Alekseeva; des. S. Akhvlediani).
First production abroad: Kleines Theater, Berlin, Jan. 1906 (dir. Max
Reinhardt); Komissarzhevskaia's Theatre on tour, New York,
Mar. 1908.
Revived: Théâtre National Populaire, Paris, 1964 (dir. G. Wilson).
First British Production: RSC, Aldwych Th., 3 Oct. 1979
(dir. Terry Hands; des. Chris Dyer; with Norman Rodway
as Protasov, Sinead Cusack as Liza, Natasha Parry as Melaniia,
and Carmen de Sautoy as Elena).
First published: Stuttgart: Verlag J. H. W. Dietz, 1905; *Sbornik
'Znanie' za 1905g*, Bk VII, St. Petersburg, 1905.
Translations: tr. A. J. Wolfe, in *Poet Lore*, Vol. XVII, No. 2 (1906), and
separately (New York: Wessels, 1912); as *Children of the Sun*,
tr. M. Budberg, Boston, 1912; tr. Kitty Hunter-Blair and Jeremy
Brooks, London, 1973, and in *Maxim Gorky: Five Plays* (London,
1988).

Pavel Protasov, an experimental scientist, his wife Elena, his sister Liza, a painter Dimitrii Vagin, and a vet Boris Chepurnoi debate the noble vocation of the intelligentsia in Russia in the eighteen nineties. Protasov, Elena, and Vagin are ready to dedicate themselves to the realization of their ideals, but Liza questions the validity of their intentions and Chepurnoi is also privately cynical. Their personal lives, however, suggest they are not as in command of their destiny as they may think. Protasov neglects his wife, who is being courted by Vagin; Liza, a nervous, hysterical young woman, long desired by Chepurnoi, constantly rejects his advances. Against these intellectuals are ranged other social groups: sundry servants, a local business man, Nazar Vigovsov, to whom Protasov is in debt; Melaniia Kirpicheva, a rich widow of a merchant who is infatuated with Protasov; and Egor, a drunkard and wife beater, who makes scientific apparatus for Protasov. The crisis comes when Melaniia offers herself and her fortune to Protasov only to meet embarrassment and rejection. Threatening to leave Elena forces Protasov to renew his attachment to her; Vagin is sent packing; Chepurnoi commits suicide. A cholera epidemic hits the community, and Egor's wife dies. In company with a mysterious acquaintance, Trosh-

chin, Egor heads a mob hunting out the local doctor as a scape-
goat. An ugly scene develops when the mob, believing Protasov's
experiments to be a cause of the epidemic, arrive at the house
to confront him. Elena draws a gun for protection, but both
Protasov avd Egor are knocked down by an odd-job man
employed by Protasov. The incident is defused, but the two sides
are not reconciled. Relieved, the Protasovs return indoors to
find Liza has gone out of her mind over Chepurnoi's death.

They're taking extraordinary measures to remove dangerous individuals,
so for example 'unknown people' appeared the other day in my friends'
rooms — for the rest of the story, look at the attached newspaper cutting.
Such ploys force me to be careful, for it would be stupid to set myself up
as a target for such scoundrels. . . . I must write to Europe of my gratitude. Even more I need to see a whole lot of people and then get on with
revising *Children of the Sun*. I must hurry. There's the trial, and then
probably prison.

Gorky, letter to E. P. Peshkova, 12-13 Mar. 1905,
SS, Vol. 28 (Moscow, 1954), p. 356

I have not the slightest doubt of the utter impossibility of staging the
work under discussion in view of its extreme tendentiousness which in
performance will excite nothing other than undesirable consequences.

Vereshchagin, censor's report,
Revoliutsionnyi put' Gor'kogo (Moscow; Leningrad, 1933),
p. 92-3, quoted in *PSS*, Vol. VII, p. 654-5

Your news has cheered me up immensely. I really didn't count on the
play passing through without 'corrections' on the part of the censor.
After your first visit to Bel'gard [Vereshchagin's superior] I sent him a
short letter. Did he talk to you about it? I just indicated that recently the
'highest authority' had so debased, sullied, and violated the people in the
eyes of Europe that to intensify all this activity with such stupid tricks as
the banning of my play would be superfluous.

Gorky, letter to K. P. Piatnitskii, 3-4 Oct. 1905,
quoted in *PSS*, Vol. VII, p. 655

Between the children of the sun and the children of the earth there exists
a no-man's land. . . . The children of the earth sense the superiority of

the children of the sun, but the creative activities of the latter say nothing to the poor, narrow, and dark minds of the former. . . . It is as if the children of the sun were blinded by the eternal glow of their ideals, as if they are swallowed up by their ideas, and they cannot take in the basic needs of those down below. . . . The play made a strong impression on those listening . . . but also caused disagreements, for the author has created all his characters with the same love and sincerity. His own sympathies towards this or that character are not clear. The play is not tendentious and for that reason gives rise to differences in interpretation.

A. Kuprin, newspaper interview after Gorky's first reading of the play to friends, *Odesskie novosti*, 14 July 1905, quoted in *PSS*, Vol. 7 (Moscow, 1970), p. 652

Just as the locksmith Egor beats his wife with a stick, so Gorky grabs a log as if it were a flail and beats Protasov and his associates about the head with it. . . . I would have understood Gorky's gibes only if, having drawn Protasov as a fanatic devotee of science, he had also shown his other side, depicting him as an example of an hypocritical pharisee who rationalizes about the greatness of knowledge and happiness, or about the good of mankind, and who, at the same time, commits a series of stupid and vile acts. . . . But his Protasov does not possess any negative characteristics. His main fault lies in his utter devotion to chemistry. And only in that.

Stark (Zigfrid), *Sankt Peterburgskie vedomosti*, 14 Oct. 1905, quoted in Iu. Grigor'ev, *'Deti solntsa': materialy i issledovaniia* (Moscow, 1947), p. 58-9

If *Summerfolk* was a slap in the face of the intelligentsia, then *Children of the Sun* was a disdainful spit in its eye. . . . The play . . . is a small box with a secret. It has to be played so that the secret of the satire is not revealed immediately. This demands great subtlety of performance and engaging artistic direction. All of this was well achieved by the Dramatic Theatre [Komissarzhevskaia's]. Subtly and unobtrusively Mr. Bravich leads Protasov to his final shaming. . . . The director has successfully balanced his production between comedy without caricature and drama without pathos.

A. P. Kugel, *Rus'*, 13 Oct. 1905, quoted in *PSS*, Vol. VII, p. 656-7

Each new play of Gorky's represents a step backwards from the previous one. *Children of the Sun* has gone further back than any. Here we have such untheatrical, unstructured, naive scenes, a formless mass, some sort of hotchpotch of romantic scenes, poised on the border between drama and farce, between beautiful poetry and dull anecdotes . . . that one simply cannot believe that all this is from the pen of an experienced and popular writer, and offered by him at a moment of intense social disturbance to those eagerly awaiting his words.

Smolenskii, *Birzhevye vedomosti*, 13-14 Oct. 1905, quoted in Iu. Grigorev, '*Deti solntsa*': *materialy i issledovaniia* (Moscow, 1947), p. 57

And now for the [Moscow] premiere of *Children of the Sun*. It was one of the tragi-comic episodes in the history of the Art Theatre. Quite early that morning rumours were already flying about town that the Black Hundreds would not permit the performance of Maxim Gorky's play. These soon developed into reports that the Art Theatre would be dispersed as a nest of revolution. Nevertheless the theatre was full. For the calming of the public, the administration of the theatre established a surveillance of the street and the yard. . . . In one fashion or another we managed to reach the last act without incident. In this act there is a . . . scene dealing with the cholera disorders. . . . When from behind the wings became audible the first voices of the advancing crowd . . . the audience was at once on guard. With the approaching din, they became perturbed, began to drone, to look round, to rise from their seats. . . . A clamour arose and outcries. . . . Hysteria broke out in the parterre, then in the upper tiers, then somewhere in the depth of the auditorium. A part of the public, thrusting out their elbows, rushed toward the exits; another section raised an outcry to persuade the timid ones that the scene was not reality but part of the performance. . . . There was jostling in the corridors, some tried to fight their way to the cloakroom, others fled as they were — with no other thought than to save themselves. . . . The most diverse shrieking din filled the theatre. . . . When calm was restored the performance continued, but the theatre had been emptied of more than half its audience.

V. Nemirovich-Danchenko, *My Life in the Russian Theatre*, tr. John Cournos (London, 1937), p. 258-63

However deep the abyss between the intelligentsia and the proletariat, however difficult it is to bridge the abyss, I fervently hope that it will be possible to build this bridge. This task is the responsibility of those who have emerged from the ranks of the proletariat, and who, having gradually risen up, have reached the peaks of knowledge. A sick society will only recover when the sources of light, beauty, and knowledge become accessible to all.

> Gorky, interviewed after visiting the Berlin production,
> *Neue Freie Presse*, 11 Mar. 1906, quoted in *PSS*, Vol. VII, p. 660

Gorky was often struck by the fact that the 'children of the sun' were people who lived through and by their interest in science and art. It was a refined life which represented, however, an ethically monstrous phenomenon against the background of millions of 'moles' living blind, dirty, tedious lives. However, in counterbalance to this, Gorky often sprang to the defence of the highest levels of the intelligentsia, declaring them first-class workers for culture. He admired great scientists and artists to such a degree that he occasionally brought reproaches on himself for his excessive love of the intelligentsia, and accusations of being over-'intelligenticized'.

> A. Lunacharskii, *Maksim Gor'kii* (1930),
> quoted in *PSS*, Vol. VII, p. 661

Can a play be considered comic in which one of the characters commits suicide, others are nearly killed on stage, and at the end the heroine goes out of her mind? . . . The irony of the play is contained in Gorky's clear portrayal of the lack of substance of the intelligentsia, its separateness from the people, its distance from life, and shows that the golden dreams of the intelligentsia about people, about the 'children of the sun' . . . will remain empty, unrealizable dreams, if the intelligentsia persists in remaining in the realm of beautiful words. . . . They must give way to someone else, side with something forceful, otherwise they will perish, for on their own they are nothing.

> B. Emel'ianov, on Tairov's production, 1935,
> *Literaturnyi kritik*, No. 6 (1937), quoted in
> '*Deti solntsa*': *materialy i issledovaniia* (Moscow, 1947), p. 75

The theatre knows very well why they decided to stage *Children of the Sun*. They decided to mount it in order to repeat with new vigour the memorable question Gorky addressed to the intelligentsia of the world in the 'thirties: 'On whose side are you, masters of culture?' . . . The participants cannot but express in the depths of the subtext their own attitudes to the present-day importunate and hypocritical hysterics of bougeois propaganda about the ideals of humanism which in reality are so foreign to the bourgeoisie. The Vakhtangov players are not updating an old play: they are simply singling out, emphasizing, and stressing its echoes of Gorky's understanding of the noble purpose of the intelligentsia's work which is in harmony with our own day. . . . Narrow, comic, and pitiful, spiritually impoverished, and encumbered with so much filth from banal, bourgeois life, Melaniia is attracted to Protasov, seeing in him her ideal of a man pure to the point of saintliness. . . . In the performance of L. Pashkova . . . Melaniia is seen as a purely comic figure, the absurdity of whose existence is striking. The role keeps revolving around the tragic inconsolability of people, dislodged from their normal niche in life. The clash between Melaniia and Protasov . . . provides one of the important themes of the Vakhtangov production.

N. Abalkin, *Pravda*, 5 Jan. 1969, p. 6

The Children of the Sun, written by Maxim Gorky in prison in 1905 and now presented by the RSC at the Aldwych, is the text-book 'intimations of the Russian Revolution' play. . . . Gorky's is a subtle and perceptive analysis and interplay of attitudes, but somehow it never quite takes wing. It remains infuriatingly in view of its many good qualities not quite a masterpiece. This doesn't mean to say that it isn't worth seeing. . . . Terry Hands's production is fluent and workmanlike.

Alan Drury, *The Listener*, 18 Oct. 1979, p. 527

The Children of the Sun may be seen as his politically revved up *Cherry Orchard*. . . . The tone, though, is far less elegiac than that of Chekhov. There's no place in Gorky for the cello-string that symbolically snaps and echoes across the cherry groves with a dying fall, because he sees little, if anything, to mourn in the disappearance of the civilization represented by his main characters. . . . Gorky's attitude to his landowner-scientist . . . is roughly what many of us might feel for some maddeningly wrong-headed yet undeniably good-hearted friend. . . . The conversation compulsively turns, as it always seems to do in Russian literature of the period, to the function of art, the future of humanity . . . then in crashes what looks like a cross between the Incredible Hulk and baleful Bill Sykes: the local blacksmith in hot and murderous pursuit of his screaming wife. . . . Just how are they supposed to evolve into the model citizens of Pavel's sun-bleached utopia? . . . It makes its prophetic points with a more than Chekhovian punch, and without wantonly blackening one class or idealizing another. These half-seeing, self-absorbed, troubled people are sharing a picnic on top of an anthill that runs ten miles deep and cannot explode anywhere but up. It's too late for boiling water or any other cure-all. Cataclysm seems unavoidable. 1917 must come.

Benedict Nightingale, *New Statesman*, 19 Oct. 1979, p. 605

Barbarians

'Scenes in a District Town in Four Acts.'
Written: 1905.
First production: Lettish Th., Riga, 26 Mar. 1906 (dir. A. Mierlauk)
Revivals: in many provincial theatres, including M. N. Solovtsov's
  company in Kiev, N. I. Sobol'shchikov-Samarin's in Kharkov,
  Basmanov's in Smolensk, 1906; Sovremennyi Th. Company, at
  Vasileostrovskii Th., Petersburg, 1907 (dir. N. N. Arbatov);
  K. N. Nezlobin's Th., Moscow, 10 Apr. 1910.
Major Soviet revivals: Kuibyshev Th., 1937 (dir. I. A. Rostovtsev);
  Voronezh Th., 1937 (dir. S. Voronov); Malyi Th., Moscow,
  31 Jan. 1941 (dir. K. A. Zubov, I. Ia. Sudakov; des. B. G. Knoblok);
  BDT, Leningrad, 1959 (dir. G. Tovstonogov; des. V. Stepanov).
First production abroad: Berlin, 12 Nov. 1906.
First British production: RSC, at the Barbican Th., London, 19 July 1990
  (dir. David Jones; with Peter Egan as Tsyganov, Mick Ford as Cherkun,
  Barbara Jefford as Tatiana, and Louise Jameson as Nadezhda).
First published: in *Varvary: drama v 4-kh deistviakh*, Stuttgart: Verlag
  von J. H. W. Dietz Nachfolger, 1906; *Sbornik 'Znanie' za 1906g*,
  Bk. IX, St. Petersburg, 1906.
Translations: tr. Alexander Bakshy with Paul S. Nathan, in *Seven Plays
  of Maxim Gorky* (New York; Oxford, 1945); tr. Kitty Hunter-Blair
  and Jeremy Brooks, in *Gorky: Five Plays* (London: Methuen, 1988).

*The arrival of two engineers, Tsyganov and Cherkun, at a small
Russian town to bring the railway creates social and emotional
havoc among the existing order. Tsyganov soon recognizes an
old flame in Lydia, who is staying locally with her aunt Tatiana.
He is quickly diverted, however, by Nadezhda, the semi-
bohemian wife of the local excise officer, Monakhov. Cherkun no
longer loves his wife, Anna. They all rent a house from Tatiana,
next door to the local mayor and timber merchant, Redozubov, a
dreaded figure locally, whose grotesque treatment of his children
soon leads to a quarrel with the new arrivals. Anna decides to
leave for a trial separation from her husband, who is attracted
to Lydia, and pursued by Nadezhda in her search for a 'hero'.
Monakhov suggests a malicious bet to Tsyganov that he will fall
in love with Nadezhda. Act 3 celebrates Tatiana's birthday and
marks Anna's return after two months of unbearable separation*

from Cherkun. Nadezhda's long-standing admirer, the local doctor Makarov, is being driven to drink by her inattention to him. Redozubov's son and daughter spend more time with the engineers than at home. In Act 4 Redozubov, his paternal and social authority undermined, tries to reclaim his daughter from the influence of the new people. The fulfilment of the bet has riven Monakhov with jealousy, while Makarov in despair arrives with a revolver to shoot Tsyganov. He misses, only grazing Tsyganov's finger, but is dumbfounded to discover that Nadezhda has fallen for Cherkun. Cherkun treats her as a joke and publicly rejects her. She takes the gun and shoots herself off-stage, but in sight of Tsyganov and Monakhov. Cherkun and Tsyganov are blamed for the catastrophe.

He depicts the manners of a small provincial town, half forgotten, where live small, half-dead people who are dull and naive like savages. Onto this barely living corpse swoop predatory kites, the railway construction engineers. They are the 'barbarians' of culture, ravenous predators who possess nothing but their appetites. . . . People of the future are also seen in this play who are the builders of new forms of life, but their turn has not yet come and their strengths are not yet known.

> N. Serebrov (A. N. Tikhonovyi), review of the unpublished text,
> *Molodaia Rossiia*, No. 1 (4 Jan. 1906), in *PSS*, Vol. VII, p. 665

What was black as black in *Summerfolk* has faded significantly in *Barbarians*. . . . The author is still seeking for an artistic formulation for his . . . reactions to the intelligentsia who are alien to him.

> A. E. Red'ko, *Russkoe bogatstvo*, II, No. 5 (1906), p. 106,
> quoted in *PSS*, Vol. VII, p. 665

In the whole play there is one character who is so remarkable that she becomes etched into the memory. . . . The wife of the excise officer Nadezhda Polikarpovna Monakhova . . . has about her an aura of genuine Russian strength and freedom. She is half-bourgeois and has read too many novels; she knows many love stories and all of them are like 'a young girl's dreams'. She speaks calmly, simply, with assurance, ponderously, and a little figuratively like a bourgeois. She is confident of her intelligence, and can neither think nor talk of anything but love. . . . She is strangely and beautifully whole: she possesses a power which both attracts and repels. . . . It seems to me as if the whole play was written for this character. This is a real 'human being': the real heroine of the play in the absence of a hero.

> A. Blok, ' O drame', *Zolotoe runo*, Aug.-Sept. 1907,
> and in *Sob. soch.*, Vol. 5 (Moscow, 1971), p. 158-9

Have *Barbarians*, put it on but . . . it is an old and heavy play. . . . If you do decide to put it on, take care with Monakhova. She sincerely believes in a great, ardent, and pure love. She believes she will find a hero who is worthy of this love. She falls in love with Cherkun at first sight; she loves his fearless eyes, his abrupt movements. She thinks she has found her hero! . . . In the final, act she cannot believe she has made a mistake, but when she is convinced that she has, then at that moment her heart dies. . . . This play is the dream of a mad writer.

> Gorky, letter to N. D. Krasov, actor and director at Petersburg Th.,
> late 1907, quoted in *SS*, Vol. 29 (Moscow, 1929), p. 46-7

Over the endless rolling expanses of rural 'straw Russia' has grown a small-town 'wooden Russia'. It has spread over the suffering country like so may boils and sores. . . . What in fact does go on in a small district town in Russia? It is a tiny but festering centre of despicable double exploitation. Cruel and unyielding primary accumulation of the most revolting kind takes place. The life blood of tens of thousands of impoverished, rough peasants is sucked out by those who sweat as if sitting round the samovar. Small-time capitalists are bred here, and their capital, which brings evil disproportionate to its size, cannot provide even that relative benefit that gives capital an historical value. All kinds of state officials shelter here: small, thin tentacles, which then merge together into a hungry provincial bloodsucker of the great all-Russian octopus. . . .

[Cherkun] energetically tears down 'wooden' Russia. . . . He is drunk with the process of great work, with the process of destruction, with the process of creating a colossal iron Moloch. But beside him stands cynical, rotten Tsyganov, and it is he who places a human content into the iron framework being created by Cherkun — a cynical depravity and a cynical plundering. . . . The old and wooden is broken down and something new corresponding to an 'iron' culture, coldly and inhumanely displays its worst instincts, and does not offer one drop of warmth and light. What if Cherkun sings the praises of the big city? What if he has great energy and strength? He is only an unconscious weapon in the hands of the blind elements of capitalism. . . . For that reason he does not possess, nor ever could, a shred of the heroism that Nadezhda is seeking so desperately. . . . If hopes are still living in the depths of 'wooden' Russia, then it is not given to the heroes of the age of steam and steel to fulfil them.

A. Lunacharskii, Vestnik zhizni, 10 Apr. 1906,
and in Sob. soch., Vol. 2 (Moscow, 1964), p. 30, 33, 34

The play depicts the same milieu as Ostrovskii had done in his time: the patriarchal-bourgeois, merchant, and bureaucratic class: a 'realm of darkness'. One or two people in *Barbarians* (for example the Redozubovs, father and son) bear a close relationship to Ostrovskii's characters.

B. V. Mikhailovskii, Dramaturgiia M. Gor'kogo epokhi pervoi
russkoi revoliutsii (Moscow, 1955), p. 201

G. Tovstonogov interpreted *Barbarians* as a tragicomedy, also characteristic of his other productions. . . . In *Barbarians* he was challenging the genre interpretation given to the play by the Malyi in the 'forties. That production, measured and colourful, was artlessly romantic. Tovstonogov's version was much more sober and strict. At those points where the Malyi went for a true, powerful melodrama, Tovstonogov called for out and out farce, which was in fact not at all alien to the play's tragic motifs.

Istoriia sovetskogo dramaticheskogo teatra,
Vol. 6 (Moscow, 1971), p. 151

The subtext of *Barbarians* was clearly shown in the production of the BDT in Leningrad. From the beginning G. A. Tovstonogov's interpretation . . . was surprising, even perplexing: in the rhythm of the play and in the intonations of the actors, and particularly in the detailed working out of the subtext to the roles, one felt a move away from Gorky towards Chekhov. But gradually the true aim of the production became clear and revealed something new in *Barbarians* and in Gorky's drama in general. The play seemed to speak with the whole of its aesthetic structure: just look how complex and multilayered are the human natures Gorky depicts and how many layers have to be removed from some of them before we reach their core! Redozubov can seem just a 'greedy gob' . . . but this gob (the role played by V. P. Politseimako) hangs open not so much from greed as from surprise and terror at everything that is going on in a social order that had seemed only recently so unchangeable. . . . Tsyganov is usually played as a spiritual bankrupt, capable only of destroying everything around him with his unbridled cynicism. Gorky's sentence on Tsyganov is merciless. But this lack of mercy is expressed in the fact that Tsyganov experiences — too late! — his first genuine, powerful feeling. The performer of this role, V. I. Strzhel'chik, did not idealize his hero; he revealed his love as an egotistic and malicious passion, similar to Monakhova's love. But because this passion overtakes Tsyganov and because this love comes to him when he no longer has the spiritual strength for it, it becomes a punishment, a torture, and a death sentence.

B. Bialik, M. Gor'kii: dramaturg (Moscow, 1977), p. 200-1

It is a slippery play to hold and at the end, while we have come to know something of the inhabitants of the small riverside Russian town, brutalized, ludicrous, or crafty as they variously are, Gorky's intention in presenting them to us remains far from clear. The play advances towards the inevitable last-minute pistol shot like a camera slowly altering focus. . . . Gradually we are asked to see that it is he [Cherkoon] and his partner, the gently born Tsyganov . . . who are the destroyers, the barbarians of the title, confusing, unwisely educating, or falling inappropriately in love with the locals, scarring the place as surely as their iron rails are destined to do.

Jeremy Kingston, The Times, 2 Aug. 1990

There is nothing shrill or propagandist about his work. If he does not have Chekhov's munificence of spirit — who does? — he can write with generosity about the nob classes and with unsentimentality about the poor.

'His curiosity and fascination with people is so intense,' says [David] Jones, 'that even the weakest and most repulsive come across as startling, fresh, and original on the stage. They have a point of view to put and put it.'

The effect is of richness, abundance, and unpredictability. Hidden feelings burst into the open, making it clear how much has been subtextually seething. The tone veers from the comic to the painful, the absurd to the ugly.

'It is a mixture you get in Chekhov', says Jones, 'but bolder, laid on with oils not water colours. You get belting great laughs at incredibly poignant devastating moments.'

That volatility, he thinks, helps explain why Gorky has been neglected in Britain. English audiences resist mood-swings so extreme, and performers find them hard to play.

Benedict Nightingale, interviewing David Jones,
The Times, 30 July 1990

The term 'barbarians' seems a little strong: Attila the Hun did worse things, surely, than ply a nervous kid with a glass of Chartreuse. And the town is no Eden for them to slither into: for one thing, almost every man — the mayor, an old tramp, the timber merchant — is accused at some point of beating his wife.

Lynne Truss, *Independent on Sunday*, 5 Aug. 1990

Gorky's writing has the ambivalence of evenhandedness: he was always a better visionary than a playwright. His real importance lies in being a passionate witness rather than an artist. . . . Gorky's problem is that he can draw pictures but can't portray events. . . . Gorky is objective enough to see the aggressiveness of one side and the primitive venality of the other, but he cannot dramatize the clash, only show the result. . . . This is one of those problematic plays: it is important but unsuccessful, its conception being more impressive than its execution. David Jones directs it with . . . a complete mastery of Gorky's rough laboured genius.

John Peter, *Sunday Times*, 5 Aug. 1990

Enemies

'Scenes.'

Written: 1905-06.

First production: Kleines Theater, Berlin, 16 Feb. 1907. The play was banned in Russia, but performances which ignored the ban included E. Riz's company, Poltava, 22 Feb. 1907 (dir. P. M. Armatov-Riz).

Major Soviet revivals: Iaroslavl', Nizhnii Novgorod, 1917; Workers' Th. of the Vasileostrov Region, Petrograd, 1918; Workers' Th. of Soviet Latviia, 1919 (dir. A. Mierlauk, who also played Pechenegov); Pushkin Drama Th., Leningrad (dir. B. M. Sushkevich; des. B. M. Khodasevich); Teatr MOSPS, Moscow (dir. Rubin; des. A. F. Bosulaev); MAT, 10 Oct. 1935 (dir. V. Nemirovich-Danchenko and M. N. Kedrov; des. V. V. Dmitriev; with V. I. Kachalov as Zakhar Bardin, O. Knipper-Chekhova as Polina, and A. K. Tarasova as Tatiana); Malyi Th., 30 Oct. 1937 (dir. K. Khokhlov; des. M. Z. Levin).

First British production: RSC at Aldwych Th., London, 22 July 1971 (dir. David Jones; des. Timothy O'Brien and Tazeena Firth; with Philip Locke as Zakhar Bardin, Brenda Bruce as Polina, Helen Mirren as Tatiana, John Wood as Iakov Bardin, and Mary Rutherford as Nadia).

Major revivals abroad: MAT on tour to Paris Exhibition, 1937; Lincoln Centre Company, New York, 10 Nov. 1972 (dir. Ellis Rabb).

First published: as *Vragi*, Stuttgart: Verlag von J. Dietz Nachfolger, 1906; *Sbornik 'Znanie' za 1906g, Bk. XIV*, St. Petersburg, 1906.
Translations: tr. A. Bakshy and P. Nathan, in *Seven Plays* (New Haven; Oxford, 1945); tr. M. Wrettlin, in *Five Plays* (Moscow, 1956); tr. Kitty Hunter-Blair and Jeremy Brooks (London, 1972), and in *Gorky: Five Plays* (London: Methuen, 1988).

Zakhar Bardin and Mikhail Skrobotov are joint owners of a textile factory. Skrobotov has been on leave and feels Bardin has been too lax with discipline. The workers have demanded the dismissal of an unpleasant foreman, but Skrobotov is reluctant to concede, and a strike is brewing. Summoned to a confrontation, Skrobotov is shot, and dies. Bardin closes the factory. Some of the Bardin family are friendly with the workers and are torn apart by this decision. The house and garden are put under guard, the troops and investigating police called in. Bardin agrees to reopen the factory if the assassin is handed over. The family begins to split: Bardin's brother Iakov, Iakov's actress wife Tatiana, and their niece Nadia are ranged against Zakhar, his wife Polina, an army general uncle, Pechenegov, and Skrobotov's widow Kleopatra and his brother Nikolai. A political agitator, Sintsov, who has been mobilizing the workers, is a particular friend of Tatiana. A substitute is provided for the real assassin. The authorities arrive and the investigation takes place. The workers are rounded up, Sintsov is recognized, and the workers' ploy to save the assassin for further political work is uncovered. Nadia, whom the Bardins have vainly attempted to silence, sides with the workers at the end of the play as they are being taken off to prison to await their trial. In Gorky's rewritten ending of 1933, Nadia's final outburst is made less vehement in favour of a declaration from one of the older workers that they would never be silenced.

I've written a three-act play, *Enemies* — not bad, rather jolly. All the same it's not the really good play I will write some day.

Gorky, letter to A. Amfiteatrov, Sept. 1906, quoted in *Gor'kii i russkaia zhurnalistika nachala veka: neizdannaia perepiska* (Moscow, 1988), p. 79

47

In these 'scenes' the irreconcilability of the enmity between the workers and the employers is vividly portrayed. Moreover, the former are depicted as staunch fighters consciously moving towards an identified aim — the destruction of capital; while the latter are shown as narrow-minded egotists. . . . These scenes are nothing but a diatribe against the propertied classes, and as a result cannot be given permission for performance.

Censor's report, 13 Feb. 1907,
quoted in *Teatral'noe nasledie*, 1 (Leningrad, 1934), p. 223

However offensive it may be, we must establish the fact that Gorky has come to a halt in his development. . . . The workers who are foregrounded by Gorky are very untypical. . . . Gorky has revealed his lack of dramatic sensitivity and complete incomprehension of the laws of writing for the theatre.

B. Brazolenko, *Vestnik znaniia*, 2, 1907, p. 120-1,
quoted in *PSS*, Vol. VII, p. 678

Gorky's new scenes suffer from a crudeness, primitiveness, and triviality in their fundamentals which mark the so-called plays written for popular theatre.

A. A. Izmailov, *Birzhevye vedomosti*, 11 Jan. 1907,
quoted in *PSS*, Vol. VII, p. 678

The creative artist is not a publicist. He does not rationalize, he depicts. The artist who depicts the class struggle must show us how the spiritual cast of mind of the characters is determined by that struggle and how it determines their thoughts and feelings. In a word, such an artist has to be a psychologist. And Gorky's new work . . . satisfies demands of this kind. *Enemies* is interesting precisely in a socio-psychological sense. . . . Whatever the period, the fact is that the intelligentsia is more inclined to rely on the 'individual', while the politically aware worker relies on the 'mass'. From this difference come two different strategies. And Gorky's *Enemies* provides a rich source for a correct understanding of the psychological basis of the workers' strategy. . . . The workers, he shows us in *Enemies*, are full of the highest self sacrifice. . . . Remember . . . the scene where Levshin and Iagodin suggest to the young worker Riabtsov that he should claim reponsibility for the murder of the capitalist Mikail Skrobotov. . . . What can be greater than the self-sacrifice of Riabtsov? And how noble are the motives of his older comrades, who show him the way to the deed. . . . They are heroes without any doubt. But they are heroes of a particular kind: they are heroes from among the proletariat. . . . They say that this work has not had much success in Berlin, where *The Lower Depths* ran for many performances. I am not surprised. A well-portrayed vagrant can catch the interest of the bourgeois art lover. A well-portrayed politically aware worker must provoke a whole series of the most unpleasant thoughts.

G. Plekhanov, *Sovremennyi mir*, 5 (1907),
and in *Izbrannye filosofskie proizvedeniia*, Vol. V
(Moscow, 1958), p. 509-27

His turn towards the proletariat was seen most of all in *Enemies*. Despite its proletarian character, this play has not even now been accepted on our stage. . . . The play is exceptionally interesting in its theme and as an indication of the author's mood. Its structure juxtaposes the individualistic and tawdry world of the bourgeoisie in all its forms with the united proletarian mass in which not only is the substitution of one man for another possible for the good of their common cause, but in which we also have before us a tightly knit collective.

A. V. Lunacharskii, *Maksim Gor'kii*, 1928,
and in *Sob. soch.*, Vol. 2 (Moscow, 1964), p. 150

A particular fuss was made when Gorky went over to Bolshevik literature in writing *Mother* and *Enemies*. . . . If this had been propaganda in general then he might have been forgiven, but this was Bolshevik propaganda. . . . Plekhanov's reproach that Gorky had incorrect ideas is quite understandable. At that time Plekhanov was an exceptionally clearly declared Menshevik, and Gorky's ideas evidently rubbed him up the wrong way.

A. Lunacharskii, *Literatura i iskusstvo*, 4 (Oct.-Dec. 1931),
and in *Sob. soch.*, Vol. 2 (Moscow, 1964), p. 127-8

I must confess to you that in my work on *Enemies* I have come to see you anew as a dramatist. You take a piece of an era which has the strongest of political situations and you examine all this not by a series of external events but by means of a typical group of well-drawn characters placed in clever formation as in chess. . . . At the same time your play provides material and sets the pattern for a particular style, and, if one may so express it, a style of a high realism. A realism of clear simplicity and great truth, expressing great typicality, the realism of a magnificent powerful language and an idea infused with pathos.

V. Nemirovich-Danchenko, letter to Gorky, 4 Feb. 1936,
Teatral'noe nasledie, Vol. 1 (Moscow, 1952), p. 140

We know very well where we are going. We already have models of the
new art: for example, *Enemies*. Our new kind of theatre is felt throughout
almost all the play. There's nothing accidental here, no groping for a
new way. . . . What are we approaching our fortieth anniversary with?
Are we the theatre of Chekhov? No, not the theatre of Chekhov. . . . That
is what struck a large number of emigrés in Paris. . . . They were angry.
In an article with a typical title, 'To the Memory of the Art Theatre',
someone wrote: 'What has come is not Chekhov's but Gorky's theatre'.

> V. Nemirovich-Danchenko, speech to MAT, 2 Nov. 1937,
> *Izvestiia*, 26 Oct. 1938,
> quoted in *Rozhdenie teatra* (Moscow, 1989)

The significance of the production of *Enemies* put on by V. I. Nemirovich-Danchenko in 1935 (produced by M. Kedrov) was enormous both
for the Art Theatre and for the stage history of Gorky's plays. . . . It
showed new possibilities for the development of Soviet theatre as a
whole. Gorky's idea that class is not something external pinned on a
person like a label, but rather what that person is, was magnificently
explored in Nemirovich-Danchenko's production.

> *Istoriia sovetskogo dramaticheskogo teatra*, Vol. 4
> (Moscow, 1968), p. 34, 38

In *Philistines* and *Enemies* he displays representatives of the proletariat:
that force which would stand up to the ruling classes in all their forms. It
was here that the confrontation was being created, the resolution of
which would lead to the future, to the overthrow of capitalism and to a
socialist society.

> B. Mikhailovskii and E. Tager, *Tvorchestvo M. Gor'kogo*
> (Moscow, 1954), p. 105

What makes the production such a satisfying whole is David Jones's
perception that the title defines the play. It isn't just the opposing classes
that are embattled. The workers display a saintly solidarity, but the ruling
class itself is torn by internal hatred: the decaying gentry loathes the
thrusting, greedy technocrats who, in their turn, despise their ineffectual
gentility.

> John Peter, *Times Educational Supplement*,
> 30 July 1971, p. 16

Though Gorky's intellectual sympathies are with the aspirations of the cloth-cap chaps, he devotes most of his attention to the predicament of the Bardin family, decent country gentlefolk with no stomach for tyrannizing their employees: well-meaning liberal humanists doomed to be swept aside as the militant socialists and harder-line capitalists come to death-grips. One Bardin brother [Iakov] is shrewd enough to have sensed which way the wind is blowing, but is too feeble in spirit to do more than offer a defeated commentary as he disintegrates alcoholically on the sidelines like a fly dissolving in acid; and John Wood . . . gives a performance so masterly that it might easily have disastrously unbalanced the ensemble. That it doesn't is due to David Jones's direction, loving and lucid, discreet and detailed. . . .

> Kenneth Hurren, *The Spectator*, 31 July 1971, p. 184

Mary Rutherford has the most difficult female part in the play: the bluestocking teenager who becomes the spokesman for the author. I am in two minds about this performance. On the surface it is brilliant: this girl has all the intensity of the frustrated spinster-to-be which is already present in the bespectacled young girl; the shrillness, the childishness and petulance, the mixture of naivety and intellectual sharpness are all here. And yet — and that is where my hesitation comes in — all this makes the girl, who surely is meant to be sympathetic, well-nigh unbearable as a human being; one recognizes the portrait as a true likeness of a character who is bound to get on one's nerves and prejudice one against any ideas such a person might advocate.

> Martin Esslin, *Plays and Players*, Sept. 1971, p. 45

Gorky does not entirely avoid the dangers inherent in portraying a group of workers . . . but he nevertheless succeeds in evoking sympathy for the young dignified Grekov, the elderly sage Levshin, and others. At the end of the Royal Shakespeare Company's 1971 production, the audience was deeply shocked when bags were unceremoniously thrust over the heads of the workers by the secret police and they were summarily executed, a detail which is not present in the text of the play but which is fully justified by the whole tenor of the interrogation with which the play ends. . . .

It has become commonplace in Soviet criticism to emphasize Gorky's enormous influence on Soviet drama and to view him as its precursor. In fact, this is a distortion of Gorky's role in Soviet drama (and Soviet literature in general) in the 1920s. Throughout that decade theatres demanded plays with a modern setting and Gorky was seen as essentially old-fashioned and almost totally ignored. . . . It was only in the 1930s that Soviet theatres rediscovered Gorky's early plays and gave

them a prominent place in their repertoires along with the new cycle of
plays which he had begun to write.

Robert Russell, *Russian Drama of the Revolutionary Period*
(London, 1988), p. 20, 22

The Last Ones

'Play in four acts', originally entitled *The Father*.
Written: 1907.
First production: Letnii Th., Tashkent, 18 June 1908; banned on
 23 June by the Petersburg censorship committee: there was,
 however, one more production at Obshchedostupnyi Th.,
 Vladivostok, 10 Aug. 1908.
Revived: Kutaissk Th., 16 Oct. 1910 (dir. M. Koreli, in defiance of ban).
Major Soviet revivals: First Moscow Workers' Th. (dir. A. A. Brenko)
 and Artists' Collective of Moscow and Petrograd (dir.
 I. A. Rostovstsev), Nizhnii Novgorod, 1917; I. Ia. Franko Th., Kiev,
 1932 (dir. K. Koshevskii; with A. Buchma as Ivan Kolomiitsev);
 Central Moscow Th. of Water Transport, 1936 (dir. A. P. Dol-
 zhanskii); Riazan' District Th., 1957 (dir. V. N. Tokarev); MAT,
 1971 (dir. O. Efremov); Moscow, 1976 (dir. Iu. Zhigul'skii).
First production abroad: Kammerspiele, Berlin, 6 Sept.1910
 (dir. Max Reinhardt; with A. Bassermann as Ivan Kolomiitsev).
Revivals: Russian Drama Circle at the Intimnyi Th., Prague,
 23 Apr.1913.
First published: as *Poslednie: p'esa v chetyrekh deistviiakh*, Berlin:
 Bühnen- und Buchverlag Russischer Autoren I. Ladyschnikow, 1908;
 Sbornik 'Znanie' za 1908g, Bk. XII, St. Petersburg, 1908.
Translations: none located.

*An assassination attempt on the life of Ivan Kolomiitsev, the
local police chief, has led to the arrest of Sokolov, suspected of
revolutionary activity. Kolomiitsev is renowned for his brutality
towards political prisoners. A public outcry at the lack of hard
evidence for Sokolov's arrest has forced his resignation pending
the trial. Kolomiitsev and his family live with his brother Iakov,
who is dying from heart trouble. The family survives largely
though Iakov's generosity. Ivan's corruption extends to his private
life, his money long squandered on women and gambling. There
are five children. Alexander, the eldest, is intent on bribing his*

way into the police force. Nadezhda is married to a doctor, and both scheme to obtain as much money as possible from Iakov. Liubov', deformed from being dropped when a baby by Kolomiitsev in a drunken rage, as it turns out is not Ivan's but Iakov's child by Sofiia, the mother. The two youngest children are slowly discovering the extent of their father's corruption: Petr joins a local revolutionary circle, and Vera elopes with a young friend, Iakorev, who betrays her trust and rapes her. Sokolov's mother begs Sofiia to intercede with Ivan and persuade him to admit there is doubt whether Sokolov was the assassin. Glimpsing the possibility of bribing his way to appointment in another town, Ivan refuses, fearing his reputation for ruthlessness may be compromised and the post be lost. On hearing of this refusal, Iakov, now supported by Liubov', withdraws the money for the bribe and instead bails Sokolov out of prison. Iakorev claims a dowry for Vera, but is renounced by her when she arrives hard on his heels and begs her parents for help. Enraged, Ivan refuses to accept that he is the cause of his children's corruption. Overcome by these angry outbursts, Iakov dies from a heart attack. Over his body, Ivan begins a speech on the sanctity of the family, is silenced, and leaves supported by Aleksander and Nadezhda, but rejected by Sofia and the younger children.

Here's a play for you: I am not sure whether or not it's successful. Personally I am unclear about it. . . . Of course it won't be possible to put it on in Russia. . . . I should like you to submit it to Reinhardt or another director already translated, as a manuscript, not forewarning them of the content or the theme. Can you do that?

> Gorky, letter to I. Ladyshchnikov, 15-16 Sept. 1907,
> quoted in *PSS*, Vol. 13 (Moscow, 1972), p. 501

The failure of *The Father* doesn't upset me, for I know myself that it wasn't a very good attempt. Leave it on ice, maybe I'll go back to it one day. Correcting mistakes is a harmful occupation.

> Gorky, letter to I. Ladyshchnikov, 19 Oct. 1907,
> quoted in *PSS*, Vol. 13, p. 501

Red, left-wing, distorting, and provocative literature. . . .

> *Rossiia*, 21 May 1908, quoted in *PSS*, Vol. 13, p. 502

All that we have are vain attempts at denigrating the police. . . .
    Novoe vremia, 28 June 1908, quoted in *PSS*, Vol. 13, p. 502

A betrayal of art. . . . Perhaps Gorky may be excused by his socialism? But where is it in the plays (*Barbarians, Enemies, The Last Ones*)? Gorky has the psychology of a provincial small businessman in its most typical form, and nothing more. Gorky's focus is his criticism of the bourgeoisie and all its props, including the police. Should we defend the bourgeoisie? When and where has a true artist ever done that? Criticism of the bourgeoisie is a norm, it is general. But can we go on to talk at the other extreme of the poetic strength and fruitfulness of democracy? Alas! these two eternal enemies are surprisingly cognate and close when it comes to matters of artistic creativity, to admiration of poetic inspiration and to the evaluation of poets. . . . An extreme democrat is a brother to the fattest 'bourgeois' in matters of art.
    Ellis (L. L. Kobylinskii), *Vesy*, No. 7 (1908), p. 57, 58

This is nothing more than a disconnected list of agonizing observations on miserable Russian life. . . . A painful evening with which one doesn't wish to associate either Reinhardt's theatre or the name of Gorky. . . .
    Vossische Zeitung (Berlin), 1910,
    quoted from *Birzhevye Vedomosti*, 28 Aug. 1910,
    in *PSS*, Vol. 13, p. 504

Although one can say a lot against the play . . . the writer was and remains a poet. . . . His poetic soul is felt in the best parts of the play.
    Berliner Tageblatt, 1910, quoted as above

The only representative of the revolutionary camp is Sokolova, the mother, who only appears twice on stage. But her interview with Sofia and Ivan Kolomiitsev is central to the play. Offstage, in the background, the figures of her son and the other revolutionaries are sketched in. Relations to events taking place off-stage, to the revolutionary movement and its participants, are constant themes of the dialogue taking place on stage. This or that position in relation to these (revolutionary) forces or unseen partners (such as Sokolov, the son) in many ways defines the pattern of the conflicts between the characters on stage.
    B. V. Mikhailovskii,
    Dramaturgiia M. Gor'kogo epokhi pervoi russkoi revoliutsii
    (Moscow, 1955), p. 348.

The Last Ones and *Vassa Zheleznova* are united . . . by their common theme. In these plays, the first of which was originally called *The Father*, and the second given the sub-title *The Mother*, the question of the stability of the family was posed. . . . Moreover, the family conflicts are depicted by Gorky as a reflection of class conflicts, the decline of the noble and bourgeois 'species' is seen as a reflection of the decline of the whole bourgeois and gentry social group, already shaken by the first Russian revolution. . . .

In connection with the Kolomiitsev children I want to mention the interesting and original production of *The Last Ones* which took place in 1976 in the Moscow TIuZ directed by Iu. Zhigul'skii. It began with the idea that the title applies to the whole Kolomiitsev family, especially to its youngest members. . . . In Zhigul'skii's production the tragic experience of the young Kolomiitsevs, Petr and Vera, is important, not only as the confirmation of the words Sofia says to Ivan: 'You have destroyed the children' . . . words which apply equally to those revolutionaries who have perished because of Ivan as to his own children whose minds and hearts have been corrupted. In this production the main idea behind the interpretation was precisely this destruction of young minds. . . .

B. Bialik, *M. Gor'kii: dramaturg* (Moscow, 1977), p. 264, 279

Gorky's accomplishments in the play are twofold. First, he has written a political play without political characters. The accused revolutionary never appears on stage. Thus the cause he represents primarily serves as a kind of litmus test to define individuals through their reaction to it. Second, Gorky has simplified and sharpened the intrigues. Instead of the complex interweavings of his earlier plays, a single main conflict, that between two brothers, predominates. If *Enemies* marks the end of Gorky's first period of play writing, then *The Last Ones* opens the second.

Barry P. Scherr, *Maxim Gorky* (Boston, 1988), p. 57

Eccentrics

'Scenes.' A play in four acts.
Written: 1910.
First production: New Dramatic Th., St. Petersburg, 7 Oct. 1910.
Revived: I. E. Duvan-Tvortsov's Company, Solovtsov's Th., Kiev, Oct. 1910; Karalli-Tortsov's Company, Khar'kov, Oct. 1910.
Major Soviet revival: BDT, Leningrad, 1962 (dir. A. D. Nikitin; with V. A. Sokolovskii as Mastakov).

First production abroad: in Russian, by amateur group of political
emigrés, Paris, 3 Dec. 1910.
First production in English: as *Country Folk*, Long Wharf Th., New
Haven, Connecticut, Feb. 1970.
First published: as *Chudaki: Stseny*, Berlin: I. Ladyschnikov Verlag,
1910; as *Sbornik tovarishchestva*, St. Petersburg: Znaniia, 1910.
Translation: as *Queer People*, tr. A. Bakshy with P. Nathan, in *Seven
Plays of Maxim Gorky* (Yale; Oxford, 1945).

*Mastakov, a writer, and his wife Elena have taken lodgings in a
house in the forest somewhere in provincial Russia. They share
it with a doctor and his father, Nikolai and Vukol Potekhin.
Nikolai loves Elena from afar, while Mastakov has fallen for a
wealthy neighbour Ol'ga. Another young neighbour, Vasia,
dying of consumption, is cared for by his fiancée Zina, who no
longer loves him, and her mother Medvedeva. The focal point of
the play is Mastakov's relationship with his wife Elena: he
describes it as one between mother and son, largely because of
his infatuation for Ol'ga, who continually badgers him to marry
her. Mastakov is exploring the theme of motherhood in his
writing and defends his credo of only writing of the good and
the positive. Appearing steadfast and strong, though at great
personal cost, Elena attempts to oust her rival by pointing out to
her how temperamental and childish Mastakov really is. Knowing of Mastakov's infidelity, Potekhin tries to save Elena from
her husband, but she rejects his offer. The death of the unhappy
Vasia relieves Zina of her burden of guilt: it also releases the
doctor from his patient, and allows him to leave for distant parts
to seek consolation for his unrequited love for Elena. A final
confrontation between Elena and Ol'ga over Mastakov follows.
Elena wins Mastakov after Ol'ga has overheard him fantasizing
to Zina about his love for her. Mastakov threatens to leave in
search of peace and quiet for work. He then reaffirms his love of
life and his desire to be positive amid all the aging minds he
sees about him, asking Elena to forget his indiscretions. She
selflessly agrees.*

Mastakov: Always sincere. He speaks very simply, unsentimentally,
unaffectedly, and always looks people in the eye. Irritable, helpless, and

slightly comic. Eloquent gestures, agile body. He's flirtatious, but not knowingly. When he listens to what people are saying he puts his head on one side and looks at them out of one eye like a bird. . . .

Elena: Loves her husband wholeheartedly and sincerely, and is convinced that in her position she could not do otherwise. She also knows that in this game sooner or later she will be the loser. Her restraint is external, inwardly she burns passionately. She is very supple, and simply, elegantly dressed.

> Gorky, 'Notes for Actors', published with the play,
> quoted in *PSS*, Vol. 13, p. 87

I have just come from the New Theatre from *Eccentrics*. . . . Success is in the balance: (i) it wasn't full; (ii) the applause was 'sceptical'; (iii) conversation in the interval was acid. Who is to blame? In the first place, the actors; in the second place, the actors; and in the third place, the actors. . . . Rybakov as Mastakov gave a competent performance. But what a part! What speeches, what conflicts! He gave us not one jot of its depth. . . .

But what a glorious play! What a fabulous woman Elena is ! How happy-go-lucky, unsystematic, talented, and life-like Mastakov: the Russian artist to a tee. . . . I could see Knipper as Elena, Stanislavski or better Kachalov as Mastakov. . . . A good picture needs a good frame, an interesting play needs good performers.

> S. A. Poperek (S. Nedolin), letter to Gorky, 7-8 Oct. 1910,
> quoted in *PSS*, Vol. 13, p. 511-12

Perhaps Gorky wanted to give a picture of his relationship with his reading public in this play. He is the one writer who has continued to sing a hymn to life, while the Russian intelligentsia, broken and disappointed, has turned away from it.

> *Kievskaia miysl'*, 3 Oct. 1910, quoted in *PSS*, Vol. 13, p. 512

Something dreary, grey, and Chekhovian . . . [Mastakov] lives outside life, in a world of golden fantasy words about a fairytale life and people, and at the same time deceives his wife, tells lies, and over the dead body of a young rebel cynically seduces his fiancée.

> F. M., *Iuzhnyi krai* (Khar'kov), 9 Nov. 1910,
> quoted in *PSS*, Vol. 13, p. 510

Your review of the play *Eccentrics* among other things said: 'Over the dead body of a young rebel a writer cynically seduces his fiancée.' . . .

Do you really consider such a phrase just? Does Mastakov 'seduce' 'cynically'? And are you suggesting that every young man who has been in prison is inevitably a 'rebel'? . . . I have only made this point because in my view the Russian writer in general deserves a more careful attitude to his work and thoughts, a more careful attitude than the one he is afforded at present which in no way promotes growth of his respect for people.

Gorky, letter to editor of *Iuzhnyi krai*,
quoted in *PSS*, Vol. 13, p. 510-11

The characters of *Queer People* [*Eccentrics*] are all intellectuals, and inevitably there is a great deal of talk concerning the problems of life, but Gorky's own attitude towards his characters has noticably mellowed. Although he calls them queer, he presents them in a warm, sympathetic light, and he clearly admires the selfless devotion of his principal heroine, Elena, as much as he forgives the indiscretions of his hero, the writer Mastakov, whom he even uses as his mouthpiece to express his own affectionately cheerful view of Russia and her people.

A. Bakshy, 'The Theatre of Maxim Gorky',
Seven Plays of Maxim Gorky (1945), p. 8

Mastakov . . . may be a self-analytical representation of Gorky himself. Mastakov writes stories that disregard obvious facts for the kind purpose of bringing cheer and comfort to his readers, and that disturbs the Russian intelligentsia, because they require him to believe in something imaginary. . . . The dramatic delight of Mastakov is his comic self-centredness. When Elena's 'well-intentioned' friends keep forcing her to confront him with his sins, he heads her off by telling her first how happy he is with her, and how he loves her with a nice quiet love as if she were his mother.

Henry Hewes, *Saturday Review*, 7 Feb. 1970, p. 24

Country People is funny, but not through 'laugh lines', rib-tickling gimmicks, or gags. A group portrait, it does not idealize human beings nor does it demean them. There is mockery in the play . . . but . . . informed with understanding, not just 'forgivenness'.

At its centre stands a writer, a silly ass about women, an idealistic conceited creature who is also a man of respectable gifts, a lover of life, a child whose folly will benefit his fellows. His wife's devotion to him — and what a fine figure of a good woman Gorky paints in her — is not misplaced. All the other characters are drawn with the same simple incisive strokes and truthfulness. Like most of the better Russian writers,

Gorky was keenly aware of his country's backwardness, and yet was ennobled by his love for it. His play is neither provincial nor 'dated'; it is just as much about us as about 'them'.

Harold Clurman, *The Nation*, 9 Feb. 1970, p. 157

Gorky undoubtedly 'endowed' Mastakov with some of his own treasured ideas about writing, but he endowed him with them precisely because a man with such a character and such a position must reveal all the hidden dangers in these ideas. . . . He put not only his treasured ideas but also his abberations into Mastakov as he tried to understand their basics and free himself from them. . . .

The stage history of *Eccentrics* is scant. In the production at the BDT . . . Mastakov was as if divided into two parts, which showed him as a positive, almost heroic figure in his creative work, but as negative, almost farcical in his private life. As Mastakov, the talented actor V. A. Sokolovskii caught all the changes in the character very skilfully, rising at moments of creative inspiration to the heavens, and falling in the dirt under the influence of minor passionate impulses.

B. Bialik, *M. Gor'kii: dramaturg* (Moscow, 1972), p. 308, 333

Gorky perhaps overdraws [Elena] in his zeal to portray a woman of towering strength and nobility. Harbouring no illusions about Mastakov, Elena draws sustenance from his youthful optimism and zest for life, and this is what doubtless also redeems him in Gorky's eyes. . . .

H. Segel, *Twentieth-Century Russian Drama*
(New York, 1979), p. 21

The work's most complex figure . . . is Mastakov. On the one hand he tries to offer his readers 'goodness and beauty'. . . . In his own life, though, he often acts irresponsibly. . . . For all his contradictions and at times absurd egotism, Mastakov remains one of Gorky's more profound dramatic creations.

B. Scherr, *Maxim Gorky* (Boston, 1988), p. 68

The Reception

'A comedy in one act', originally entitled *Children*.
Written: 1910.
First production: Solovstov's Russian Th., Kiev, 13 Oct. 1910.

Revived : Workers' Theatre Group, Educational Institutes House, Petersburg, 1914 (dir. P. P. Sazonov).

First published: as *Deti: komediia v odnom deistvii*, Berlin: Bühne- und Buchverlag Russischer Autoren I. Ladyschnikow, 1910; as *Vstrecha*, in *Sovremennyi Mir*, No. 9 (1910).

Translation: none located.

Zobnin, a merchant, has organized a ceremonial welcome in a station waiting-room with vodka, wine, and titbits for the local prince, who is about to arrive by train and from whom Zobnin wishes to buy some forest for his timber yard. His preparations are interrupted by another merchant, Kichkin, who is bent on the same purpose. They decide to join forces and become business partners in the venture, but their plans are upset by other visitors for the prince, including an old woman with a petition, a drunken guard, an inventor, and an alcoholic passenger who misses his train. The Prince has in fact already negotiated the sale of the forest with a German business acquaintance, who is accompanying him, and after the hospitality they quickly leave. The despondent merchants drown their sorrows in an impromptu party.

The vaudeville seemed all right to me, perhaps even funny in places if it were played as a farce. I think you wrote it with that in mind. Will it be published? If so, then if I have time, could I put it on in our cabaret? This year we want to put on some of Maupassant's one-acters and other things like that.

> L. A. Sulerzhitskii, letter to Gorky, Aug. 1910,
> quoted in *PSS*, Vol. 13, p. 517

It's a farce, quite an artistic one, and that's how it should be played. . . . [This] was played without style. In fact, it is uncertain what was played, but it was crude. . . .

> P. Iar(tse), *Kievskaia mysl'*, No. 274 (4 Oct. 1910),
> quoted in *PSS*, Vol. 13, p. 518

A cumbersome piece. . . .

> M. Rabinovich, *Teatr i iskusstvo*, No. 42 (17 Oct. 1910),
> quoted in *PSS*, Vol. 13, p. 518

I have read *The Reception* and am in ecstasy. Let me put it on either at the Art Theatre, or in a theatre of one-act plays which I want to get going next year. . . .

> K. Stanislavski, letter to M. F. Andreeva, 15 Apr. 1911,
> *Sob. soch.*, Vol. 7 (Moscow, 1960), p. 521

There are many real-life touches in Gorky's play, and it is all underpinned by a vivid, at times even crude, humour. Gorky the master craftsman of old is present in some of the characterization.

> S. T., *Den'*, No. 46 (16 Feb. 1914), quoted in *PSS*, Vol. 13, p. 518

Stanislavski's theatre of one-act plays was not founded. . . . In addition there was the situation which caused even Gorky to remain aloof from *The Reception* (also from *The Zykovs*): when the First World War began, the play with its negative portrayal of a German could have been staged as part of a wave of chauvinistic fervour.

> B. Bialik, *M. Gor'kii: dramaturg* (Moscow, 1977), p. 343

Vassa Zheleznova

First Version

'A Play in Three Acts'; 'The Mother: Scenes'.
Written : 1910. Awarded the Griboedov Prize, 1911.
*First production : *K. N. Nezlobin's Th., Moscow, 21 Feb. 1911; group from New Dramatic Th., Zimnii Buff Th., Petersburg, 13 Mar. 1911.
Major Soviet revivals: Troupe of the Town Education Department, Ivanovno-Voznesensk, 1918; Collective Farm Th., Leningrad, 14 Feb. 1935 (dir. V. F. Dudin; des. Rudi and Kriuchkov); Shevchenko Th., Kharkov, Dec.1935 (dir. L. E. Dubovik; des. D. I. Vlasiuk); Stanislavski Th., Moscow, 1978 (dir. A. Vasil'ev; des. I. Popov; with E. Nikischikhina as Vassa).
First production in English: BBC Radio 3, 11 Nov. 1986 (dir. Matthew Walters; with Billie Whitelaw as Vassa).
First published: as *Vassa Zheleznova: p'esa v trekh deistviiakh,* St. Petersburg: Teatr i iskusstvo, 1910; as *Vassa Zheleznova, Mat':* *tseny,* Berlin: Bühnen- und Buchverlag Russischer Autoren I. Ladyschnikow, 1910; *Sbornik 'Znanie' za 1910g,* Bk. XXXIII, St. Petersburg, 1910.

Translations: tr. A. Bakshy with P. Nathan, in *Seven Plays of Maxim Gorky* (Yale; Oxford, 1945); as *Vassa Zheleznova: a Mother*, tr. Tania Alexander and Tim Suter (Oxford, 1988).

The Zheleznov family are rich builders' merchants. Since Zakhar, the father, is dying, Vassa, the mother, summons home her married daughter Anna to help unite the family round the business: but Zakhar's brother, Prokhor, and Zakhar's sons Semen and Pavel are threatening to pull out their capital. As the fiscal bonds are breaking, sexual and moral corruption begin to emerge. Zakhar had mistresses; Anna's army husband is a drunkard and her children are bastards; Prokhor is having an affair with Liudmilla, who when pregnant had been hastily and conveniently married off to Pavel, a cripple, and with Prokhor's help had aborted the child. Semen's wife Natalia has sexual fantasies of herself as a siren in heaven; Lipa, the servant, had a son by Semen but strangled it. Vassa, determined to retain control of the business, blackmails Lipa to poison Prokhor. Lipa fails and then hangs herself. On the day of Zakhar's funeral, Vassa and Anna create a family scandal by egging Pavel to attack Prokhor in a fit of frenzied jealousy. Prokhor collapses, and Anna administers an overdose of pills on the pretext that he is having a heart attack. To discount Semen's and Pavel's claims on the business, Vassa then produces a new will in which Zakhar has left sole control to her. She blames Pavel for Prokhor's death and decides he must go to a monastery to escape police detection — thus liberating Liudmilla, whom she admires, from her enforced marriage.

It's that fathomless, dark maternal instinct, the beginning of all life. In my view you've created something great. I want to say thank you in the name of art.

M. M. Kotsubinskii, letter to Gorky, Dec. 1910, quoted in *PSS*, Vol. 13, p. 522

From an aesthetic point of view, in its clarity and power the figure [of Vassa] recalls Ibsen's heroines. . . .

V. Tikhonovich, *Rul'*, 6 Dec. 1910, quoted in *PSS*, Vol. 13, p. 523

At Nezlobin's *Vassa Zheleznova* was performed with great verve. Not for nothing did the audience shout for the performers so fervently.

Moskovskie vedomosti, 17 Feb. 1911,
quoted in *PSS*, Vol. 13, p. 522

A woman with an exceptional mind and an iron will, Vassa Zheleznova does not balk at any methods for achieving her goal. . . . Only she draws the attention and even the sympathy of the reader, because in her alone . . . is there a sense of someone who can love but who cannot find anyone or anything to love.

V. P. Kranikhfel'd, *Sovremennyi mir*, No. 1 (1911), p. 363,
quoted in *PSS*, Vol. 13, p. 523

An unnecessary and unreal accumulation of all kinds of crime. . . .

S. A. Vengerov, *Russkie vedomosti*, No. 1 (1 Jan. 1911),
quoted in *PSS*, Vol. 13, p. 523

This is some kind of 'abyss'. . . . Gorky's play is a dark story, an episode of a criminal nature, not a typical representation of everyday life. . . . There is nothing profound to draw from this crime-centered play.

K. Arn (Arabazhin), *Solntse Rossii*, 18 (Mar. 1911),
quoted in *PSS*, Vol. 13, p. 524

In the end what is the basic idea of this play? Perhaps the author wanted to show the decay and disintegration of a bourgeois family? Very probably, but why did he then place Vassa, whose actions repel us, in such a sympathetic light?

Ben (Nazarevskii), *Moskovskie vedomosti*, 17 Feb. 1911,
quoted in *PSS*, Vol. 13, p. 525

Wealth becomes an aim in itself, an absolute life task. . . . The striving for money is not fuelled in the end by a maternal instinct, but it is the striving itself which forces on Vassa the need to become a mother, that is to have 'legal' heirs. Her children are good for nothing, so she looks for ready-made heirs to her fortune: ' . . . Let my sons depart. I shall live for my grandchildren.'

V. V. Vorovskii, *Zvezda*, 6 Jan. 1911,
quoted in *PSS*, Vol. 13, p. 526

There are strong men of different alloys in all Gorky's plays; strong women, too, busy at first in seeking strong men for mates; but as time went on and disillusion grew with the pioneers that the democracy had sent before them into the middle class (see in particular *Villa-folk* [*Summerfolk*], 1903, and *Children of the Sun*, 1904), the strong men were gradually ousted by strong women, careful mothers providing for the future. . . . In *Vassa Zheleznova* (1911) the wheel has gone full turn and men are nowhere. . . . The path of a Gorkian strong mother is plain. . . . Quite shocking, according to any moral or criminal code hitherto discovered, but definite and downright, demanding an answer; and withal excellent art, informed by that breath of life which dull critics call technique. . . .

George Calderon, *The Quarterly Review*, No. 432 (1912), p. 26

The designer I. Popov (1978) created an ugly, cluttered interior. At the back of the stage there were pigeons in an actual pigeon loft: the only glimmer of real vibrant life. At first seeming slow and narrative, this production had its own inner tension and tautness. Rich, individual details produced great effects, such as, for example, the scene of Prokhor's death. His heart attack was brought on by white, whispy feathers from his beloved dead pigeons being thrown at him.

V. A. Maksimova,
Istoriia russkogo sovetskogo dramaticheskogo teatra,
Vol. II (Moscow, 1987), p. 189-90

Like other merchants in Gorky's work of the time, [Vassa] has good sides that mitigate her less attractive qualities. The sub-title *Mother*, which recalls Gorky's novel of the same name, indicates that for all her rapacity she can be protective toward those she loves. . . . The conflicting qualities within her raise Vassa to the stature of a tragic figure. She is guilty of much wrong, but often she was inspired by a desire for the good. . . .

B. Scherr, *Maxim Gorky* (Boston, 1988), p. 100-01

Counterfeit Coin

'Scenes'. A play in three scenes.
Written : 1913/1926.
First production: in Italian, by Tatiana Pavlova's troupe, Rome and
    Naples, 1928-29.

First production in USSR: in Yiddish, Jewish Th. in Bielorussia,
1937-38 (dir. V. Golovchiner).

Major Soviet revivals: Vladivostok Dramatic Th., on tour to Moscow,
July 1955 (dir. K. Vedernikov; with G. Antoshenkov as Iakovlev,
M. Poletaeva as Polina); Gor'kii Dramatic Th., 1958 (dir.
M. A. Gersht; with N. A. Levkoev as Iakovlev and E. V. Suslova
as Polina); Malyi Th., 1972 (dir. B. A. Babochkin; des. T. Livanova;
with S. A. Makrushev as Iakovlev and A. S. Potapov as Efimov).

First publication: as *Fal'shivaia moneta: stseny*, Berlin: Verlag Kniga,
1927 (sub-titled 'written in 1913').

Translations: none located.

---

*A moral piece in melodramatic form which through the meta-
phor of forgery explores the complex issue of truth and falsehood. It centres on one-eyed Iakovlev, a watchmaker, who lives
with his second wife Polina, his daughter Natasha, and his niece
Klavdiia in the house of Kemskoi, a legal official. Part of the
ground floor serves as Iakovlev's shop. A stranger comes to rent
some rooms, but is recognized by Polina as Stogov, her first
lover – and cause of her earlier arrest, trial, and imprisonment.
Stogov offers to supply Iakovlev with forged gold coins. Kemskoi
has given the house to Natasha, and it is quickly confirmed that
she is his natural daughter and not Iakovlev's. Polina begs her
husband to send Stogov away, for her fear of him may drive her
to kill him. Iakovlev refuses, saying she must be responsible for
her own sins. At the revelation that Natasha is not his daughter,
Iakovlev dissolves into manic laughter, claiming he had known
all along, and turns to drink. The forged coins have the power
of distinguishing genuine from false people. At Stogov's sug-
gestion, Natasha leaves one on a table and Glinkin, her fiancé,
takes it: she then refuses to have anything further to do with
him. Polina, still in love with Stogov in spite of herself, is
rejected by him, and leaves the house. Luzgin, a frequent visitor
whose purpose in life is to seek out lost inheritors of fortunes is
near insanity, haunted by his own reflection in a mirror. After
causing a major row, he is overpowered by Stogov, but his
ravings are prophetic: he claims that money is the root of all
evil, and news is brought that Polina has committed suicide,
thowing herself under a train.*

Stogov: officer in the criminal investigation department. He's come to town to find counterfeiters. . . . He's a decent man, but there's something dark in his past — an error rather than a crime. . . . He's indifferent about himself, like someone who has lost what is most precious to him. He doesn't like police work. He's condescending towards other people . . . [but] feels sorry for Polina. . . .

Luzgin: insane, that sums him up. However, that doesn't make him dramatic in the first two acts. He's funny, but not a caricature. . . . In his past there is an incident in which his son suffered and in which a crucial role was played by a woman. He's a private investigator, and is really looking for heirs to escheated property. . . . The meaning of the play can be found in Stogov's words . . . 'You can distinguish real people from false ones only by putting your mark on them. But this spoils them.'

Polina: her attitude to Stogov at the beginning is one of a woman who has been ignored by him and who no longer believes him, but she does develop the hope that perhaps Stogov really does want to help her. . . . In my view the pace of the play should not be slow, and the comic elements should be emphasized.

> Gorky, letter to Eric Boehme, his German translator, 1926,
> in *SS*, Vol. 12 (Moscow, 1952), p. 460-1

Falsehood is the main character in the play. . . . Five minutes do not pass without someone uttering a lie or a lie appearing before you.

The madman who seeks an heir for escheated property . . . is a . . . symbol, which must be expressing the writer's idea that truth has been lost, and perhaps does not even exist at all. . . . Unless you take this play symbolically it loses its value, and would not have been worth even the writing. . . . Even if it is taken as broadly symbolic, the play will satisfy hardly anyone. . . . When you write a symbolic play, which incorporates 'life in general', how can you remain silent about the existence of the revolution and all its ideas and slogans and its building for the future? . . . My personal view is that this play is totally unnecessary to our theatre and adds nothing to Gorky's fame.

> A. Lunacharskii, *Krasnaia gazeta*, 18 Nov. 1926,
> quoted in *PSS*, Vol. 13, p. 537-8

I have read Lunacharskii. . . . The play was written in 1913, and Lunacharskii asks why there is nothing about the revolution in it. . . . Oh dear!

> Gorky, letter to V. I. Khodasevich, 28 Nov. 1926,
> quoted in *Novyi mir*, No. 3 (1968), p. 44

What has happened? Has Lunacharskii not passed my play? Nor will the Germans be putting it on, it seems. They are afraid. It's awkward to put on a play which has been panned by the Minister of Public Education.

Gorky, letter to E. P. Peshkova, 17 Jan. 1927,
quoted in *PSS*, Vol. 13 (Moscow, 1972), p. 539

The play, as readers of my article will remember, rather upset me. . . . It seems I was badly misled. Reliable sources have informed me the play *Counterfeit Coin* was written in 1913. . . . Of course, in such circumstances the play must be approached from quite a different point of view and all that I wrote about it was incorrect.

A. Lunacharskii, open letter to *Krasnaia gazeta*, 20 Jan. 1927,
quoted in *PSS*, Vol. 13, p. 540

I am not writing a commentary to the play. It's not what I usually do. I have written something and readers have the right to take what I have written any way they wish. I do not consider I have the right to say how what I write should be understood.

Gorky, letter to Oscar Gellert, his Hungarian translator,
10 Jan. 1927, quoted in *PSS*, Vol. 13, p. 541-2

M. Teif (1937) gave us an excellent translation into Yiddish. But the production was too eclectic and stylized in its detail. . . . Gorky's play was treated as a melodrama.

Istoriia sovetskogo dramaticheskogo teatra, Vol. 4
(Moscow, 1968), p. 640

Counterfeit Coin is perhaps the one play of Gorky's our theatres have neglected unjustly. . . . The director K. Vedernikov and the performers have tried to convey the atmosphere of a stifling, corrupt bougeois world. . . . In the world of the Iakovlevs, the Glinkins, and the Luzgins everything is subordinated to the thirst for profit and wealth. Here everything is rotten, or has taken on repulsive forms: people's attitudes to the family, and to others close to them. Everything is eaten up with hypocrisy and lies. . . . G. Antoshenkov is oustanding. . . . He portrays Iakovlev as a cunning, insidious man looking everyone over with his one eye: what can he get from them? Can he get rich at their expense? There is something tragi-comic that is both terrifying and funny in this character. He examines Stogov closely for a long time, and when the latter suggests he should make counterfeit coins, how the old man livens up!

He is haunted by the gold, lots of counterfeit gold, which he will have! . . . However, Gorky does not only portray cruel and stupid people. He also wished to project good and honest people . . . who are seeking a way out of this repulsive company. Even though a tragic fate awaits Polina as she dies in the concluding part of the play, her character is shot through with a yearning for real life. M. Poletaeva conveys Polina's complex feelings with restraint and tact. . . . One thing is without doubt, the Vladivostok Theatre has brought to the stage one of Gorky's most complex plays. And for that they should be praised.

V. Frolov, *Pravda*, 10 July 1955, p. 2

In 1958 at the BDT . . . the play was presented as a tragi-comedy. True, at isolated moments the search for comedy became too obvious, which told on the performance even of such an experienced and talented actor as N. A. Levkoev. In his interpretation Iakovlev sometimes became too shallow and pathetic . . . but on the whole he and the rest of the performers (E. V. Suslova reached great heights of tragic pathos as Polina) uncovered the complex content of Gorky's characters. . . .

Babochkin created a production (1972) after which the dispute over whether or not *Counterfeit Coin* was or was not necessary to our theatre has become a matter of the past. In this production both the comic and the tragic hearts of the play were revealed in equal depth. The characters of that 'pillar of morality' Iakovlev (S. A. Makrushev) and his 'double' Efimov (A. S. Potapov) demonstrated not only that in the bourgeois world is it one step from the terrible to the laughable, but also that in this world it is but one step from the laughable to the terrible . . . a world in which even a fire is better than the daily boredom which stifles everything; a world in which insanity is better than ordinary soul-destroying mediocrity; a world in which the normal is in fact most abnormal — such is the incontrovertible reality of bourgeois existence, which the Malyi theatre production conveyed in a remarkable way.

B. Bialik, *M. Gor'kii: dramaturg* (Moscow, 1977), p. 370-1

In the large dingy house with its cramped and crooked cubby holes of rooms (des. T. Livanova, 1972) everything was pushed up together, even absurd. Every character was like a thick-bottomed glass. Life was disturbing and confused as in a dream. A mirror placed on the front of the stage served as a means for the characterization and self-discovery of the characters. It forced them to stop suddenly and abruptly, look hesitantly at their reflection, and react to it in different ways. The hopeless search conducted by Luzgin (D. Pavlov), unable to find anyone to whom to give a large inheritance, took on symbolic meaning: there are no heirs in this life, which hovers over an abyss of threatening catastrophe. Even the inheritance itself might turn out to be 'counterfeit coin'.

V. A. Maksimova,
Istoriia russkogo sovetskogo dramaticheskogo teatra,
Vol. II (Moscow, 1987), p. 188

The issues at the heart of the play are such as to suggest the influence of the greatest Italian dramatist of the time, Pirandello. While Gorky's original conception may have owed something to Pirandello's stories, his reworking of the play brought it closer in spirit to Pirandello's major works of the 1920s, most notably *Six Characters in Search of an Author* (1921); we should recall that both versions were completed during periods when Gorky was living in Italy, and he no doubt was familiar with Pirandello's work.

B. Scherr, *Maxim Gorky* (Boston, 1988), p. 72

The Zykovs

'Scenes.' A play in four acts.
Written: 1912-13.
First production: Narodnyi dom, Petrograd, 6 July 1918
(dir. N. P. Arbatov).
Major Soviet revivals: Pushkin Academic Th. of Drama, Leningrad,
1940 (dir. N. Simonov); Red Torch Th., Novosibirsk, 1944
(dir. Vera Redlich; with V. Kapustina as Pavla); Moscow Dramatic
Th., 1952 (dir. V. Dudin).
Productions in English: Equity Library Th., Master Th., New York,
17 Oct. 1974; RSC at Aldwych Th., 28 April 1976 (dir. David Jones;
with Paul Rogers as Zykov and Mia Farrow as Pavla).
First publication: as *Zykovy: stseny*, Berlin: I. Ladyschnikow Verlag,
1914.
Translations: tr. Alexander Bakshy with Paul Nathan, in *Seven Plays of
Maxim Gorky* (Yale; Oxford, 1945); and in *The Lower Depths and
Other Plays* (Yale, 1945).

*Two concepts of love which are opposed and irreconcilable also
reflect a generation conflict. The action of the play, which is set
in the Volga region, begins with a betrothal party for Mikhail
Zykov and Pavla, a rather strange, convent-educated innocent.*

However, Mikhail's formal proposal of marriage is rejected by Pavla in favour of one from Antipa Zykov, his father, who is reliving the passionate experiences of his youth, but seems to Pavla to offer protection and security as well as wealth. However, very soon after their marriage, Pavla's view of love as harmonious coexistence is challenged by Antipa's passionate attraction to her. She cannot understand Antipa's objections to her affection for Mikhail, to whom she increasingly turns out of boredom. Unable to master his jealousy, Antipa neglects himself and his business. His sister Sofia begins to take over. She has two suitors — Muratov, a forester, whom she despises, and Hevern, a German, who flatters her and becomes a partner in the business, but systematically cheats her brother. Pavla's admission of her affection for Mikhail brings father and son into direct conflict, with Antipa brandishing a gun. Sofia intervenes, allowing Mikail to escape with the gun. Mikail then attempts suicide. The devastated Antipa is quickly reconciled with his son, but lays the blame on Pavla, whom he all but physically harms. Muratov in the meanwhile has provided evidence of Hevern's swindling, hoping to win Sofia for himself. But Sofia refuses them both, telling Pavla that she must grow up and take responsibility for her actions. At Sofia's urging, Antipa finds the strength to tell Pavla to leave, but in doing so breaks his heart.

I am very pleased not to give the play to the Art Theatre. Nemirovich's plan to put on *The Devils* [by Dostoevskii] is abhorrent to me. I'm going to protest in print about this propagandizing of sadism.

> Gorky, letter to I. Ladyzhnikov, 5 Sept. 1913,
> quoted in *PSS*, Vol. 13, p. 546

I do not know at all who they've got in the company [Svobodnyi Teatr/Free Theatre] or whether they will ruin the play. . . . I like your idea of going ahead and publishing the play if Mardzhanov can't do it, or I see that they have no one to act in it.

> M. F. Andreeva, letter to Gorky, 10 Sept. 1913,
> quoted in *PSS*, Vol. 13, p. 547

I do not think it is a good idea to publish the whole play, since there is a German in it from the second act onwards. He's a bit of a scoundrel.

Although the play was written in 1912, it isn't made any better by the German. Other people can make them nasty without me doing it as well.

Gorky, letter to editor of *Sovremennik*, 28 Dec. 1914,
quoted in *PSS*, Vol. 13, p. 543

Antipa represents activeness in Gorky's scheme of things, while Antipa's son represents passiveness. The great Maxim's typical 'active' heroes as we all know have titanic views of the world . . . they see humanity as nothing more than a 'louse'. The timber merchant-cum-industrialist Antipa has this kind of simplified view of things.

V. P. Burenin, *Novoe vremia*, 3 Apr. 1915,
quoted in *PSS*, Vol. 13, p. 548

A clear apology for strength, individualism, and the bourgeoisie. . . . Young Russia is . . . represented as a degenerate, rickety, talentless, and lily-livered race!

S. Timofeev, *Teatr i iskusstvo*, No. 24-25 (1918),
quoted in *PSS*, Vol. 13, p. 549

V. Kapustina . . . played Pavla so finely and so pointedly. The first appearance of Pavla in the Zykov house was reminiscent of Easter, of a peal of bells. She was all light and triumphant. There was something child-like and mysterious in her fragility. But as soon as she spoke her first words the audience were on the alert. In the second act the alertness turned to concern, into a need to understand who this girl was who felt so assured in the Zykov house. And then in the last act in front of us was a bad-tempered bourgeois, who had no understanding of love, god, or moral duty. . . .

The critics thought highly of the portrayal of Sofia created by M. Babanova (1952). They noted the finesse and gracefulness of her performance. She really brought something fresh to the part, interpreting it in an unusual way. What she produced, however, did not entirely coincide with what Gorky had created. There was was more of Babanova than Gorky in Sofia: she was too elegant and too vulnerable for a Gorky heroine.

Istoriia sovetskogo dramaticheskogo teatra,
Vol. 5 (Moscow, 1969), p. 171

Gorky is writing about a bourgeois society in a state of perilous drift. But what gives his play its guts and spirit is his feeling that all these

characters have human potential that is being fruitlessly squandered. . . .
Admittedly Gorky's writing . . . is often crude and jagged as if the words
have been hurled on the page. But . . . his plays survive through their
sheer emotional intensity. . . . If Gorky doesn't take root in the English
repertory, it certainly won't be the fault of Jones or his dedicated crew.

Michael Billington, *The Guardian*, 29 Apr. 1976

The generation conflict, mirroring the larger disintegration of the merchant class through erosion of its work ethic, is . . . the play's dramatic
centre. Zykov himself . . . asserts this contradiction between his son's
anti-social cynicism and his own useful labour. . . . The social effect is
the core of every relationship and Gorky provides a careful network of
nuances and pauses which illuminate the play's contradictions. Zykov
himself has relaxed his own life's effort in the debilitating aura of
Pavla's torpor, neglecting his business, allowing himself to be cheated
by his partner.

In this pattern of counter-relationships we have the play's dynamic
between those who move the world forward a step and those whose
lethargy erodes it. Precisely in this aspect the Aldwych production
seriously misfires, pitching itself higher than the subtle temper of the
work. The effect is to shatter its composure and upset the strategic
balance between the characters. The acting is generally overstrained,
playing into the melodrama and overriding the numerous low-key
sequences, which are Gorky's moments of intense confrontation. The
most misconceived of all is Sheila Allen's Sofia Ivanovna. She is the
play's moral centre and in her Gorky places his own hopes for a new
Russia, for change without violence, based on productive labour. Not
merely the pillar of the family, a cool businesswoman opposing corruption at every step, she also carries the drama's emotional stability. While
others are contemptuous of life or collapsing around her, she stands
always taut, optimistic, and reserved, denying her own personal happiness to ensure that of the Zykovs and to promote the best of Russian
values. . . . Jones and Allen have kept Sofia Ivanovna on the edge of
hysteria from start to finish, spilling over much too often for the original
character to survive.

David Zane Mairowitz, *Plays and Players*, July 1976, p. 21

The Royal Shakespeare Company . . . plods doggedly through the minor
works of Maxim Gorky. . . . *Summerfolk* was a great trial to the patience,
and *The Zykovs* is a commonplace family chronicle with little to com-
mend it as social comment and rather less as drama. . . .

Kenneth Hurren, *The Spectator*, 8 May 1976

The young innocent, Pavla, is really extremely selfish, demanding, ignorant, and dependent. 'The innocent eye' is not the solution to (what it always is in Gorky) 'the social problem'. Something much bigger than the Zykov brother and sister is stirring outside. But their kind of energies will be needed. In future, people will be judged by deeds rather than words, the endless Russian philosophizing of his previous plays. . . . *The Zykovs* leaves the outside world quiet and implicit, if constantly threatening, and within the symbol of the divided family stresses more the struggle between work and idleness than between exploitation and suffering. . . .

The plots of Gorky's plays tend to melodrama. But simply considering the plots, so do Ibsen's, to whom in many ways Gorky seems closer than to Chekhov. But nonetheless so dramatic; and melodrama only has a bad name when the characters and their society are not plausible. Gorky's are, for like the crowd scenes of the impressionistic masters of Paris, he paints a whole society, everything rings authentic — which is a great tribute to the producer and actors, too, for it could be stagey, or over-politicized. . . .

Gorky's audiences were not meant to be engulfed by any final strident affirmation or denunciation — the curse of most social (indeed official) art. For if the brother and sister have liberated themselves as persons, we know, not just with hindsight but by fraught symbols of social doom and decay underlying the surface action of the play, that the object of their energy, the self-respect that comes of useful work, is going to be made hideously complicated by future and conflicting criteria of socially purposive work.

Bernard Crick, Times Higher Education Supplement, 4 June 1976

[The play] is constructed like a symphony, in which there are three musical motifs, which now interweave with one another, now repulse one another. The play narrates the fates of the three Zykovs, each of whom experiences in their own way the same drama — a drama of lost illusions.

B. Bialik, M. Gor'kii: dramaturg (Moscow, 1977), p. 392

The central character, Antipa Zykov, is a lusty and earthy Russian merchant of the old school, a type first brought onto the stage in the 1840s by the playwright Aleksander Ostrovsky. Despite Gorky's patent distaste for capital and the world of mercantilism, he found himself magnetically attracted to the rough-hewn old merchants of the Zykov type. . . . Like Ostrovsky . . . he contrasted their essential humanity and proximity to the folk with the contemptuousness and spiritually bankrupt cynicism of the homegrown Russian capitalist. . . .

But in the differences that can be observed between Antipa and Sofia, I think Gorky leaves no doubt that there is more to admire in the self-sacrificing courage of the latter than in the raw strength of the former.

H. Segel, *Twentieth-Century Russian Drama*, p. 25-7

The Old Man

'Scenes.' A play in four acts.
Written: 1915.
First production: Malyi Th., Moscow, 1 Jan. 1919 (dir. I. S. Platon; des. K. F. Iuon; with S. A. Golovin as the Old Man, P. M. Sadovskii and L. A. Ryzhov sharing the role of Mastakov, O. O. Sadovskaia as Zakharovna, and V. N. Pashennaia as the Young Girl).
Major Soviet revivals: I. F. Volkov Dramatic Th., Yaroslavl, 1943 (dir. I. Rostovtsev; with P. Gaideburov as the Old Man); Kamernyi Th., Moscow, July 1946 (dir. A. Ia. Tairov; with P. Gaideburov as the Old Man); I. Ia. Franko Th., Kiev, 1967 (dir. B. Meskis, des. M. Ivnitskii).
First publication: as *Starik: p'esa*, Berlin: Ladyschnikow Verlag, 1918; and in *Peterburgskii al'manakh, 1*, Petersburg; Berlin, 1922.
Translations: as *The Judge*, with preface by Gorky, tr. M. Zakhrevsky and B. H. Clark (New York, 1924); tr. M. Wettlin, in *Five Plays* (Moscow, 1956).

Mastakov, a successful builder, is celebrating the completion of a technical school by giving a lunch for the workers. Mastakov is alarmed because strangers have been making enquiries about him, and he has recognized one of them as a past acquaintance. His grown-up stepchildren, Pavel and Tania, and his neighbour Sofia Markovna, a colonel's widow, know nothing of his past. The Old Man, Pitirim, and Young Girl turn up in the second act to confront Mastakov, the Old Man, who is claiming payment of a moral debt from Mastakov. The young girl seems dimwitted and is in some way mysteriously bound to the Old Man. Sofia Markovna's arrival prevents further revelation of their purpose. In a letter to Sofia, Mastakov reveals he had been arrested for murder in his youth, but is not himself sure of his guilt as he was drunk at the time of the crime. He was condemned to hard labour, from which he escaped. The confrontation between the Old Man and Mastakov is witnessed in secret by Sofia Markovna. The Old Man is determined to exact retribution from Mastakov for his rejection of the suffering imposed on him for his crime. There is a brawl, and Sofia is forced to reveal her presence. The Old Man had spent twelve years in prison for rape. Sofia compares the success Mastakov has made of his life with the Old Man — who, in enduring his suffering, has become capable of seeking only vengeance. Sofia, in a determined effort to establish Mastakov's innocence and obtain a pardon for him, interviews the Young Girl and tries to persuade her to leave the Old Man. She, too, has been in prison after her baby was frozen to death. Meanwhile Pavel has extracted information from the Young Girl which he passes to Kharitonov, Mastakov's business partner and father of Tania's suitor Iakov. They decide Mastakov is no longer trustworthy and that Pavel is now the effective owner of the business. Mastakov shoots himself, and the Old Man and the Young Girl beat a hasty retreat, the Young Girl in her distress at Mastakov's death cursing the Old Man.

Mastakov: about 40-45, light-coloured hair, bearded typical face of a good Russian peasant. His troubled conscience causes an uncertainty of speech, a carefulness in his movements. But when he lets go, as in the scene with the Old Man, he is terrifying. Not for long, though. On the whole he is a good, kind man.

The Old Man (Ptirim): about 60-65. Dressed in a kind of monk's clothing — a long cassock. An evil, glowering face. His movements are supple and snake-like. He pretends to be bent with age, but he can suddenly straighten up, and he is terrifying in his hatred for people. He considers he has suffered innocently and loves to make other people suffer and to torment them. This is the source of all his pleasure in life. He is a master of, and an artist in, suffering. . . .

The Young Girl: has a vacant, animal-like gaze with staring eyes. She is greedy, sensual, and stupid. She stands quite still and her lifeless eyes stare at everything and everyone.

Gorky, notes for The Judge (New York, 1924),
quoted in PSS, Vol. 13, p. 554-5

Please accept my sincere gratitude for the flattering (to me) manner in which you and Alexander Ivanovich Sumbatov [director of the Malyi

Theatre] referred to my play, which in fact was written in a hurry and is
brim full of weaknesses.

Gorky, letter to P. M. Sadovskii, Oct. 1918,
quoted in *SS*, Vol. 29 (Moscow, 1955), p. 385

O. O. Sadovskaia as Zakharovna was so natural that it was difficult to
tell whether it was acting or real.

E. N. Gogoleva, *Gor'kovskie chteniia,* 1961
(Moscow, 1964), p. 406, quoted in *PSS*, Vol. 13, p. 560

When this complex philosophical play appeared on the stage of the
Malyi Theatre in 1919 it met a situation of bitter ideological wrangling
and was interpreted in many ways by the critics, who opposed one another about many things, but were united in their inability or reluctance
to understand the ideas of the piece. According to one interpretation
Mastakov ... was a creator of the 'new life', while the Old Man ... was
utterly opposed to it in his envy, malice, and vengeance. In another
interpretation, on the other hand, the Old Man represented a spirit of
protest against bourgeois well-being, while Mastakov stood for those
bourgeois values.

B. Bialik, *M. Gor'kii: dramaturg* (Moscow, 1977), p. 415

In the hands of a less fine writer, the theme of *The Old Man* would
have only been turned into a penal drama. Not without success, Gorky
has tried to make the incident more profound and more intimately
patterned. . . . The play breathes the life of yesteryear . . . and would
have been more topical . . . [and] sensational, had it appeared not now
but at the end of 1916. . . . It would be more correct to call it *The Elder*.
For the central character in mentality and in his 'devilish' manner is
extremely close to Grigorii Rasputin, the notorious doom-ridden hero of
the end of the 'House of the Romanovs'.

A. Treplev *Vestnik teatra*, No. 2 (6-7 Feb. 1919),
quoted in *PSS*, Vol. 13, p. 555-6

Count Tolstoy has given us a whole series of stories to show how good
persists in men, though they have done evil. In *The Old Man*, Gorky's
play, we are shown the reverse of the picture: the obstinate persistence
of evil, a kind of abstract evil.

Review of Berlin publication,
The Times Literary Supplement, 24 Feb. 1921, p. 124

It is difficult to understand [the Old Man's] purpose: is he a blackmailer; an idiosyncratic seeker after truth in the manner of Dostoevskii; or, more probably, a fanatic?

K. Loks, *Pechat' i revoliutsiia*, No. 2 (1922), p. 359,
quoted in *PSS*, Vol. 13, p. 556

At the heart of the play lies a motif familiar to Gorky's readers: man is above everything; man is the measure of all things. The Old Man is the embodiment of a dry, formal, cruel, callous, inhuman, absolute justice. A justice of conscience and of truth, and which tyrannizes fanatically and without purpose.

A. K. Voronskii, *Krasnaia nov'*, No. 3 (1922), p. 267,
quoted in *PSS*, Vol. 13, p. 556

I have tried to show how repulsive a man may be who becomes infatuated with his own suffering, who has come to believe that he enjoys the right to torment others for what he has suffered. . . . When such a man has convinced himself that such is his right, that he is for that reason a chosen instrument of vengeance, he forfeits all claims to human respect. It is as if a man were to set fire to houses and whole towns simply because he feels cold.

Gorky, introduction to *The Judge*
(New York, 1924), quoted in
New York Times Book Review, 23 Nov. 1924, p. 4

If we take the play (and this is what we should be doing) just as it is, then sometimes not by force, not by design, nor by stretching a point, a very great, enormous, exceedingly important quality may be seen in it (despite its dramatic and archetectonic weaknesses). It can be projected into our own times, since all those evil beginnings which are incorporated into the Old Man, particularly his tendency towards violence, towards the enslavement of others, and to base his own welfare on the subjugation of others, are also characteristic of fascism.

A. Ia Tairov,
lecture to the Kamernyi Theatre Company, 1946,
quoted in *Zapiski rezhissera* (Moscow, 1970), p. 455

[The Old Man's] hatred for humanity is linked to his predatory greed. He has the hatred of an executioner for man, fused with a pathetic cowar-

dice as regards those in authority. The depth of Gaideburov's psychological analysis is supported by the clarity and strength he has brought to
his characterization of the part. It is one of the clearest and boldest.

S. Durylin, *Vecherniaia Moskva*, 4 July 1946,
quoted in *Istoriia sovetskogo dramaticheskogo teatra*,
Vol. 5 (Moscow, 1969), p. 164

The most open of Gorky's attacks on the ideas of Dostoevskii was . . .
his play *The Old Man*. . . . In the Old Man's opinion there is no point in
deciding who is right and who is wrong. 'Everyone is guilty', everyone
is sinful, and all are obliged to suffer. For the Old Man it is unimportant
whether Mastakov actually committed the crime for which he was sen-
tenced to hard labour. It is more important for him that Mastakov dared
'to transgress the law' by fleeing from hard labour and refusing to carry
his cross. The Old Man is not moved by the fact that Mastakov now
brings a lot of benefit to people: that's meaningless in the face of the fact
that Mastakov 'has not paid his price in suffering'. . . . And the Old Man
experiences particular malevolent pleasure in that, knowing Mastakov's
secret, he can so easily destroy everything he has built up. . . . He wishes
to have full power over Mastakov, over his property and over his soul. . . .

Mastakov's suicide is not treated by Gorky as a great feat or as a
victory over the Old Man. It is an act of weakness, not strength.

B. A. Bialik, *Gor'kovskie chteniia, 1949-50*
(Moscow, 1951), p. 454-7

Perhaps more than any of Gorky's plays, *The Old Man* shows an affinity
with one of his great predecessors in European drama, Henrik Ibsen. . . .
Ibsen often favoured a peculiar dramatic structure in which much of the
key action has taken place before the play opens — *John Gabriel
Borkman* (1896) and *Rosmersholm* (1886) are but two examples; the
same device appears in both *Counterfeit Coin* and *The Old Man*. Perhaps
most crucial, though, is the smaller cast that Gorky comes to employ.
Like Ibsen, he learns to concentrate on a handful of main characters.
While *The Old Man* has eleven characters, only four of them are of any
real importance, and the conflict ultimately boils down to just two:
Mastakov and Pitirim. By creating dramatic tension out of events that
have occurred before the play begins, and by probing the psyches of his
protagonists more deeply than before, Gorky creates a powerful
narrative, which may well have resulted from the belated but beneficial
influence of Ibsen on his dramatic technique.

Barry Scherr, 'Gorky the Dramatist: a Re-evaluation',
Fifty Years on: Gorky and His Time, ed. N. Luker
(Nottingham, 1987), p. 56-8

Egor Bulychev and the Others

'Scenes.' A play in three acts.
Written : 1931.
First production : Vakhtangov Th., Moscow, 25 Sept. 1932
  (dir. B. Zakhava; des. V. V. Dmitriev; with B. V. Shchukin as
  Bulychev); BDT, Leningrad, 25 Sept. 1932 (dir. Vl. Liutse and
  K. K. Tverskoi; des. M. Z. Levi; with N. F. Monakhov as Bulychev).
Major Soviet revivals: MAT, 6 Feb. 1934 (dir. V. I. Nemirovich-
  Danchenko and V. G. Sakhnovskii; des. K. F. Iuon; with
  L. M. Leonidov as Bulychev); Vakhtangov Th., 1951 and 1956
  (with S. Luk'ianov as Bulychev); MAT, 1964 (dir. B. N. Livanov).
Productions abroad: Otherwise Club, Barn Th., Shere, Surrey,
  17 Aug.1937 (dir. John Burrell; with Marne Maitland as Bulychev);
  Long Wharf Th., New Haven, Connecticut, 1970 (dir. Arvin Brown;
  with Morris Carnovsky as Bulychev).
Film: Egor Bulychev, 1972 (dir. S. Solov'ev, who also wrote the
  scenario; with M. Ul'ianov as Bulychev).
Translations: tr. A. Wixley, in *Four Soviet Plays* (London, 1937);
  as *Yegor Bulichoff,* adapted by Gibson Cowan, in *The Last Plays of
  Maxim Gorki* (London, 1937); tr. A. Bakshy and P. Nathan, in *Seven
  Plays* (Yale; London, 1946); tr. Margaret Wettlin, in *Classic Soviet
  Plays* (Moscow, 1979); tr. Bernard Isaacs, in *Collected Works in
  English, Vol. 4* (Moscow, 1978-80).

---

*Egor Bulychev, a middle-aged timber merchant, is dying of
cancer of the liver. His wife Kseniia, his daughter Varvara, her
husband Zvontsov, and his illegitimate daughter Aleksandra
(Shura) are all at loggerheads. Bulychev is having an affair with
the housemaid Glafira, and believes the only people who really
love him are Glafira and Shura: but he has a rough affection for
his godson Iakov Laptev, who is involved in the revolutionary
movement. The play is set in the spring of 1917, and the breath
of revolution and the disintegration of society from without
affect the household no less than Bulychev's approaching death
from within. Concerned at the rumours of political change,
Varvara and Zvontsov, with Zvontsov's cousin Tiatin and a
business acquaintance Dostigaev and his wife, are planning to
cut Kseniia and Shura out of the business on Bulychev's death.*

Desperate to find a cure, Bulychev summons various quack healers who utter oaths and a fireman who blows a trumpet, to no avail. Kseniia's sister Melaniia, an abbess, who has a considerable amount invested in the business, now wishes to retrieve her capital. Bulychev uses her visit to demonstrate his own lack of faith and her lack of purity, causing a major row. Melaniia's convent is attacked, and she seeks refuge in Bulychev's house. She brings more healers to Bulychev, one of whom, a holy fool, precipitates a crisis in Bulychev's illness. A street demonstration and revolutionary songs are heard outside. Nearing his end, and thinking it might be a requiem mass, Bulychev struggles to reach Shura at the window as she excitedly greets a new era.

Act 2. The fireman is excellent. . . . But I don't like the orchestra: you need only trumpets. . . . For a sick man Bulychev dances too much before this scene. It is very painful and difficult for him to go down on his haunches. It is a marvellous moment of bad behaviour and quite in character for him. . . . The audience will laugh a lot. The fireman . . . has a marvellous nose and just the right skinny look. It is a pity the sound cannot be stronger: he needs more power. The high-pitched trumpets get in the way. . . . I should like to say again how pleasantly surprised I am at everything the theatre has put into this play. It seems to me that such collaboration between theatre and author is extremely valuable in itself and for our time. . . .

Gorky, address to the Vakhtangov company, 19 Sept. 1932,
quoted in *PSS*, Vol. 19, p. 498-9

In *Bulychev* I was again struck by the fascinating charm of your Russian merchants, the Bugrovs and Morozovs, for example. Shchukin cured his liver with Picasso's pictures. . . . If, like Shchukin with his pictures, Bulychev could have cured himself with the trumpet, somewhere alone away from everyone, he would, I think, have believed in it with delight. The lack of faith coupled with the desire for it is so surprising in all these father figures from the past. This is probably one ingredient in the tragedy of your great 'merchant characters' and their 'attractiveness' as literary types.

K. A. Fedin, letter to Gorky, 13 Dec. 1932,
Literaturnoe nasledstvo, Vol. 70 (Moscow, 1963), p. 543

I do not quite understand, dear Fedin, how the 'charm' of my merchants can 'attract'? . . . Our literature has refrained from the merchant. For the gentry-writer the merchant was not a hero, for the *declassé* intellectuals he was a boss and an enemy. In 'exposing' the Moscow merchants, Ostrovsky was moved to admit: man may be a pig, but he is an amusing one! . . . Sometimes I think that I have managed to say something significant about this group, but if I measure what I have said against what I know then I feel despondent, for I know a great deal but am able to say little.

> Gorky, letter to K. A. Fedin, 21 Dec. 1932,
> quoted in *PSS*, Vol. 19, p. 498

The hopeless, doom-ridden fate of the most talented representatives of trading capital is revealed with such clarity! The language of the play is startling. . . .

> V. Ivanov, *Sovetskoe iskusstvo*, 44 (27 Sept. 1932),
> quoted in *PSS*, Vol. 19, p. 500

What confusion on the faces of those of our 'critics', who are used to identifying a concept of 'positivenesss' with 'absoluteness'. They cannot imagine that such an old fox as a profligate and tyrant of a merchant can carry out a relatively positive social function, even when it amounts to fundamental criticism, itself emerging from an animal-like fear in the face of death, of existing society, and the human whirlpool it creates.

> A. Afinogenov, *Sovetskoe iskusstvo*, 44 (27 Sept. 1932),
> quoted in *PSS*, Vol. 19, p. 501

Theatres had to express and incorporate into the images of art the birth of the socialist state and the spiritual world of the builders. . . . An immense role in the ideological and creative development of the theatre in [the 1930s] was played by M. Gorky: his play *Egor Bulychev and the Others*, performed by the Vakhtangov Theatre in 1932, opened a new era in the history of the Soviet theatre. . . .

Two philosophical points of view were revealed. And if Leonidov's reading (and even more so that of N. Monakhov) took us back to the nineteenth century, recalling *The Death of Ivan Il'ich*, . . . then Shchukin's interpretation had no close link to the past. His view is linked to a new understanding of humanism and to the need to affirm life: it is directed towards the future.

> *Istoriia sovetskogo dramaticheskogo teatra*,
> Vol. 4 (Moscow, 1968), p. 26, 31

In his interpretation of Egor Bulychev, N. F. Monakhov (BDT, 1932), in contrast to B. V. Shchukin (Vakhtangov, 1932), emphasized not Bulychev's love of life, but his incurable disease, seeing it as a symbol of the incurable disease of bougeois society.

PSS, Vol. 19, p. 503

Leonidov has gone along quite a different track from the one I wanted the play to follow. God knows where he got the idea from that the play is about death. About death in general. He seems to think it is like *The Death of Ivan Il'ich*. He has taken on a very gloomy tone. . . . I wanted something strong and unyielding. . . . I must tell you that I liked the Vakhtangov production very much. But here [at MAT] I wanted to take a different angle. They put in some noisy effects, clearly a pointed gesture towards newspaper politics. Our production is more academic, with the deepest possible examination of everyday life of the text, and with the greatest emphasis on the actor's art.

Vl. I. Nemirovich-Danchenko, letter to K. S. Stanislavski,
Feb. 1934, quoted in *Iz proshlogo*
(Moscow, 1938), p. 391-2

This study of a man at grips with the whole problem of existence, though because of its setting it will be taken as propaganda by the unperceptive, is the real stuff of tragedy. It is no more propaganda for or against anything than any study of human nature must be. . . . Bulichoff is never the fur-coated capitalist beloved of crude propagandists. His point of view, as to the rights and wrongs of revolution, is put with such sympathy that one sometimes marvels that the play should be tolerated in Russia. The implication that human nature will be the same whatever the system of government makes the propaganda, if such it be, dangerously double edged. . . . The craftsmanship of the play cannot be too highly praised. It is the first of an unfinished trilogy, but it is complete in itself. . . .

This production by the Otherwise Club at the Barn Theatre, Shere, is the first in this country, and is an extremely creditable one.

The Times, 18 Aug. 1937, p. 8

The only cause for doubt was the somewhat simplified treatment of Pavlin (Vakhtangov production, 1932). Unfortunately he is almost always depicted as a money-grubber and glutton, rather than as the exponent of a particular system of ideas. Of all the performers of this role I have seen, the most interesting was the actor V. Starchich, who played Pavlin in the production of the Yugoslav Drama Theatre on tour here [Moscow] in 1956. You could understand in this production why Pavlin could be elected to the Duma, just as you could understand why Bulychev could not wait to have a go at him.

B. Bialik, *M. Gor'kii: dramaturg* (Moscow, 1977), p. 495

I was afraid that [Starchich] would simply caricature the role, a simple, as often happens, external exaggeration on the basis that Gorky had not accidentally given him the name of Pavlin (peacock), endowing him with all the vanity of the peacock. But the actor created a harsh, spare, laconic image of an intelligent priest. . . .

Iu. A. Zavadskii, *Izvestiia*, 24 May 1956

[Ul'ianov in the 1972 film] emphasized the isolation of his hero. In the first scene he is shown at the station, not at home, where a convoy is arriving from the front with the wounded. Ul'ianov plays on a sad, even gloomy aloofness, projected by his whole body as he leans against the station wall (as if it were a prison). Likewise the consultation scene, when the half-naked Egor stands before his doctors, his arms raised, becomes a prison examination, not a medical, but an examination of a man condemned to death. . . .

Simplifying matters a little, it is possible to say that all the performers of Bulychev divide into two groups: on the one hand those who show him believing in the inevitability of his illness, and on the other those who show him unable to believe and refusing to give way. In each group there have been distinguished, even great actors, but real success has only been achieved by those in the second group. . . . Critics note that in Carnovsky's performance (USA, 1970) Bulychev is a strong man, even powerful, who despite his serious illness lives a full life. Since Carnovsky has gained fame as the best performer in the USA of Lear and other Shakespearian heroes, to the traditional category 'Gorky and Chekhov' American criticism has added 'Gorky and Shakespeare': Bulychev is regarded — and I am not exaggerating! — as comparable to Shakespeare's heroes.

B. Bialik, *M. Gor'kii: dramaturg* (Moscow, 1977), p. 500

The symbolism of the play's end is obvious; Bulychev's death is the death of Bulychev's Russia, of the old Russia of tradesmen, property owners, and capital. The death is no less irrevocable than the passing of the cherry orchard into the hands of Lopakhin. . . . In *Yegor Bulychov* it is the era of Lopakhin ending and that of the people's Russia beginning. . . .

Although Bulychev perceives injustice around him, his enlightenment does not extend to any real comprehension of the social events that are moving to transform the lives of everyone. It is this partial enlightenment, this incomplete rebellion, that endows the character of Bulychev with both complexity and interest.

H. B. Segel, *Twentieth-Century Russian Drama*
(New York, 1979), p. 36, 38

The parallels between the death of Egor Bulychev and the end of the society in which he flourished are inescapable and clearly intentional, yet as in each of his major works Gorky manages to avoid an over-schematic design by drawing a central character through whom he can investigate not only socio-political questions relating to a particular historical moment, but also psychological and philosophical questions of universal application. . . . Egor himself . . . is one of the great characters of twentieth-century Russian drama. Through him Gorky is not afraid to raise the unanswerable questions about life and death, and while he dismisses the facile answers of Egor's spiritual adviser, Father Pavlin, about the immortality of the soul, he is honest enough to leave the question resonating rather than give a glib answer on the social and political level, although that is where his own sympathies clearly lie.

R. Russell, *Russian Drama of the Revolutionary Period*
(London, 1988), p. 159-60

Dostigaev and the Others

A play in three acts.
Written: 1932.
First productions: BDT, Leningrad, 6 Nov. 1933 (dir. Vl. Liutse;
    des. A. V. Rykov; with K. V. Skorobogatov as Dostigaev);
    Vakhtangov Th., Moscow, 25 Nov. 1933 (dir. B. E. Zakhava;
    des. V. V. Dmitriev; with O. N. Basov as Dostigaev).
Major Soviet revivals: MAT, 1938 (dir. L. M. Leonidov and
    I. M. Raevskii; des. V. F. Ryndin; with Gribov as Dostigaev);
    BDT, 1952 (dir. N. Raevskaia); Ermolova Th., Moscow, 1952
    (dir. A. Lobanov; with V. Lekarev as Dostigaev); Malyi Th.,
    Moscow, 1971 (dir. B. A. Babochkin, who also played Dostigaev;
    with I. Liubeznov as the Bearded Soldier, N. Belevtseva as Kseniia
    Bulycheva, and K. Roek as Zhanna).
First published: God semnadtsatyi: al'manakh tretii (Moscow, 1933),
    p. 7-58.

Translation: adapted by Gibson Cowan, in *The Last Plays of Maxim Gorki* (London, 1937), some characters being omitted in this version.

The fate of some of the characters from Egor Bulychev and the Others *is determined in the months leading up to the 1917 October revolution. Bulychev's godson Iakov Laptev, now a Bolshevik revolutionary, is joined by Tiatin, suitor to Bulychev's illegitimate daughter Shura. Dostigaev adopts a policy of compromise, supporting whichever group appears to be in power. Melaniia and Pavlin, as representatives of Church authority, are discredited by their thirst for power and determination to rule through fear. Taisia, the novice, rejects Melaniia and the church, and takes a step towards the revolutionaries, represented in this play by Riabinin and Kalmykova. Others quickly become victims of the growing strength of Bolshevik power. Merchants and businessmen such as Nestrashnyi and Gubin, who formerly held power in this provincial town, find their status undermined. After an attempt to organize an armed insurrection they are arrested by the local Bolsheviks, whose leaders have just seized power in Petrograd. People's worth is now determined by their politics. Initially querulous, Shura also joins the Bolsheviks, while Antonina, Dostigaev's daughter, on the brink of marriage to Nestrashnyi's son Victor, is shocked by her own worthlessness in the new situation, and commits suicide. The Dostigaevs end the play under house arrest despite their attempt to curry favour with Iakov by intiating the arrest of Nestrashnyi and his co-conspirator Gubin.*

You must remember that Nestrashnyi is a leader of the 'black hundreds'. He has been a leader for a decade, and when he says 'they are scaring us', he is speaking of himself, of his own anxiety and of his fear as a man whose life has been turned upside down and who is being turfed out from among the 'leaders'.

Gorky, letter to B. E. Zakhava, 26 Feb. 1933,
quoted in PSS, Vol. 19, p. 509

Dostigaev is very good. In my view he does not put his hand in his pockets enough. . . . Hands often speak louder than words and can say exactly what other people ought not to know. . . . He is ironic, a sceptic. He has his own view about everything, so he has to be played as somewhat reserved. . . .

Riabinin . . . is a man who has been used to being busy from childhood. He is a good fitter. . . . He gets too angry in the scene with Melaniia and Dostigaev. He has no cause to be angry: he knows these people. . . . He tends to mock and tease a little. . . .

Laptev: he is a bit too severe. . . . He speaks calmly. Despite the fact he is young he does have experience as a revolutionary. So he does not need to shout. . . .

The Bearded Soldier: he must be shown clearly. He is an epic soldier [who] has understood that 'what we have to do is kill all the bosses' and he has come to kill them. . . . There is a touch of humour to him too. . . .

When Dostigaev has seen his daughter and comes on to the stage, something is missing. . . . The essence of the matter is not there. His daughter's death is not so serious as the thought, 'What is going to happen now?' That is what really matters. He is a man who loves life, who is capable of much. . . .

> Gorky, address to the Vakhtangov company,
> 7 Oct. 1933, quoted in *PSS*,
> Vol. 19, p. 516, 518, 519

Treat the play as if it were a comedy!
> Gorky, address to the BDT company, *Zvezda*, No. 6 (1937), p. 203,
> quoted in *PSS*, Vol. 19, p. 520

I particularly remember the Bearded Soldier. . . . There is an intentional symbolism here: the Bearded Soldier is a man who has grown up in the chains of suffering and tortured by injustice. He seeks peace, land, and work. A call to arms sounded in Gorky's voice. The People were coming.
> V. Ivanov, *Pravda*, 1 Nov. 1938,
> quoted in *PSS*, Vol. 19, p. 513

A. Lobanov's interpretation was the first really modern version of the play. . . . V. Lekarev's Dostigaev was more shrewd than any of his colleagues and less noticeable than any of them. Of medium height, stolid, with small features in a well-formed face, he could easily change his expression, and pretend. For that reason the Bearded Soldier followed him closely in the final act. The Gubins, Nestrashnyis, Chugunovs, and Antonina belonged to the past and perished with it. Dostigaev could transfer to the future, and make a place for himself and even become 'indispensable' and 'important': the production was warning of this danger.

Istoriia sovetskogo dramaticheskogo teatra, Vol. 5
(Moscow, 1969), p. 168-9

Some articles claimed that the 'system of party affiliations' recalled 1905 rather than 1917. . . . The directors of the production at the Vakhtangov Theatre (1935) spoke of the necessity of introducing some changes to the historical context of the play. They introduced readings from 1917 newspapers into the play (the newspapers were read by representatives of the various political groupings), and they requested the author to write in a special scene, where the [Socialist Revolutionaries] could be seen and where there was discussion of the Mensheviks. Gorky did as the theatre asked. However . . . he did not include this scene in the published version of the play. . . .

B. A. Babochkin's production at the Malyi in 1971 is of great importance on a matter of principle. This production . . . actively participated in the debate which had gone on since the play's first appearance. . . . In particular it rejected the idea that the main events in the play take place off-stage and that only their echoes reach the audience, and that this is not a play with its own action, but a 'panorama' in which a series of brilliant miniatures is cobbled together thanks only to the historical background. These miniatures are in fact part of the web of characterization in the play and demand from the actor the ability to play the episodic roles as major ones, of immense significance not only to the separate cameo scenes, but to the whole play. . . . I. Liubeznov managed to create from the few lines allotted to him an astonishingly real Bearded Soldier whose humour brought him to life and who, though clear of any external 'monumental' treatment, was still a genuinely epic figure. . . . K. Roek transformed the role of the count's mistress Zhanna, consisting only of one or two responses, into a masterpiece of the actor's art. . . . But the main achievement was the interpretation of Dostigaev as the most central figure in the play and as responsible for genuinely uniting the action. Babochkin's Dostigaev became not a compromiser, but someone who played the role of a compromiser who was, in fact, an active enemy of the revolution, perhaps even the most active, and certainly the most dangerous of anyone in the play.

B. Bialik, *M. Gor'kii: dramaturg* (Moscow, 1977), p. 502, 538-9

Except for Dostigaev himself, no major character appears throughout the play. Two-thirds of the cast appear only in a single act. . . . If the play has a fault, it lies in Dostigaev. His cynicism soon wears thin and in any case he is rather peripheral to what is going on. The play thus lacks a strong centre.

B. Scherr, *Maxim Gorky* (Boston, 1988), p. 99

Vassa Zheleznova

Second Version

A play in three acts.
Rewritten: 1935.
First production: Central Red Army Th., on tour to Leningrad, 5 July 1936 (dir. Teleshov; des. V. P. Kiselev).
Major revivals: MOSPS, 28 Oct. 1936 (dir. S. G. Birman, who also played Vassa; des. V. A. Shestakov); Malyi Th., 26 May 1952 (dir. K. A. Zubov and Velikhov; des. B. G. Knoblok; with V. N. Pashennaia as Vassa); TsTSA, Moscow, 1976 (dir. A. Nurdonskii; with A. Sazonova as Vassa).
Productions in English: Greenwich Th., Nov. 1985 (dir. Helena Kaut-Howson; with Janet Suzman as Vassa); Classics on a Shoestring Company, Gate Th., Notting Hill, Nov. 1990 (tr. Cathy Porter; dir. Katie Mitchell; des. Peter Ruthven Hall; with Paola Dionisotti as Vassa).
Film versions: Gorky Film Studio, 1953; Mosfilm, 1983 (dir. Gleb Panfilov).
First published: God deviatnadtsatyi: Al' manakh 9-yi (Moscow, 1936).
Translation: tr. R. Dalglish, in *Collected Works in Ten Volumes, Vol. 4* (Moscow, 1978-1980); adaptation by Kaut-Howson and translation by Porter, noted above, unpublished.

In this very different version from the original, the corruption of the bourgeois business class is almost totally unrelieved. Vassa has run the family shipping business for years, while her husband Sergei has gambled, drunk, and whored the proceeds. With Sergei now being prosecuted for paedophilia, and her attempts to hush up the affair failing, Vassa suggests he should poison himself to save the family honour. Vassa's brother Prokhor has got the maid Liza pregnant, and bribes her to spy on his sister. Vassa has two daughters — Natalia, an incipient alcoholic under Prokhor's tuition, and Liudmilla, with whom Vassa shares a common interest in gardening. Sergei takes poison and dies, but Liza has overheard Vassa's threats to Sergei. Liza is cowed into silence by Prokhor, and then commits suicide. Vassa's eldest son is dying of consumption in Switzerland. His wife Rachel has entered the country illegally to claim her son Kolia, who had been left in Vassa's care. Vassa refuses to yield her grandson on the grounds that Rachel cannot provide a secure existence for him. As Rachel had taken her son, so Vassa is now claiming Rachel's. Prokhor and Natalia, in hatred of Vassa, agree to a plan to kidnap Kolia, but Rachel, acknowledging she still has important revolutionary tasks to accomplish, decides to leave her son where he is. Unwell, Vassa returns home from a business crisis and arranges for her secretary Anna to report Rachel to the police. She then has a stroke and dies. Anna steals as much as she can from the safe before summoning help. Prokhor will control the business as he is guardian to Vassa's children. Rachel can only pose the question which closes the play: what do Prokhor and his kind really own?

[The MAT Company have written to Gorky] with a request to make some additions to the [1910 version of the] play which will bring it more in line with contemporary reality. . . .

Komsomol'skaia pravda, 8 May 1935,
quoted in *PSS*, Vol. 19, p. 524

Please stop rehearsing. In January I'll give you a completely new text with new characters. I do not see any sense in putting the play on in its present form.

Gorky, telegram to I. N. Bersenev, director at MAT,
Iskusstvo i zhizn', No. 3 (1938), p. 11,
quoted in *PSS*, Vol. 19, p. 525

What is this new play of Gorky's about? It is about that fearful, vile life of pre-revolutionary Russia. . . . The play begins exceptionally power-fully. The very first scenes depict an atmosphere thick with corrupt family morals. Events pile up, the spring of theatrical action is wound ever tighter, people's characters are revealed in ever greater depth.

I. N. Bersenev, *Pravda*, 19 Jan. 1936,
quoted in *PSS*, Vol. 19, p. 526

Watching the play you begin to understand why Stalin found Gorky so dangerous. Rachel condemns Vassa as a slave to the system she controls. But this obeisance to Marxism is far less powerfully projected than the Strindbergian horrors of Vassa's marriage to a drunken ex-sea captain guilty of corrupting minors or the comic depravity of Vassa's wastrel brother who tries to lure women to his room to inspect his collection of locks. Vassa is a lonely workaholic who sacrifices everything to the cause of profit: her daughter-in-law ia a dedicated puritan ready to sacrifice her child to the cause of revolution. Today, they both seem like victims of a merciless ideal. . . .

As the evening progresses, [Janet] Suzman is increasingly compelling. She prowls round her bare-boards drawing room like a house detective, emits odd flashes of motherly concern as if her true nature has been warped, and is astonishing in the final scene when the energy visibly drains from her, and her head describes a slow arc as she sinks into death.

Michael Billington, The Guardian, 18 Nov. 1985

In her programme note Helena Kaut-Howson lists exhaustive changes and additions in the 1935 version. But Gorky's main intention was clearly to bring the piece politically into line by elevating Vassa's family to the rank of wealthy class enemies, and supplying them a revolutionary opponent, so as to transform a struggle over private inheritance into an ideological combat.

The Greenwich production is a conflated adaptation of both texts, but, whatever liberties the director has taken, Vassa clearly emerges as a masterpiece transcending any schematic intention. The most obvious proof of this is the figure of the heroine herself, a character who totally defies moral judgement.

Irving Wardle, The Times, 18 Nov. 1985

The play . . . permits Janet Suzman to give as relentlessly an unsentimental performance as I've seen on a British stage. . . . She makes you feel that the most damaged of victims is herself. . . .

Benedict Nightingale, New Statesman, 6 Dec. 1985

The second *Vassa Zheleznova* is a badly flawed work. All the drama is concentrated in the first act and at the end of the third. Between them stretches a morass of directionless talk. Rachel's many allusions to 'the cause' and 'a dying class' are maddeningly obtuse, her Jewishness and her socialism quite unexamined. Most damagingly of all, Vassa's collapse and death are inexplicable. We know that she is a Zheleznova, a woman of iron, only by marriage, but it is patently Gorky's need to bring these formless ramblings to an end that causes her to give up the ghost so suddenly. . . . Panfilov's development [in the Mosfilm of 1983] of the role of Onoshenkova is fitfully alluded to. Liudmilla in the 1935 version is replaced by Pavel, who is played by and as a ten-year-old child. The result of these tamperings is to exaggerate the play's inherent implausibilities and introduce inconsistencies.

Julian Graffy, *Times Literary Supplement*, 6 Dec. 1985

Paola Dionisotti gives a knockout performance as the ship-owning matriarch in Gorky's study of Tsarist decadence: makes you understand why there was a communist revolution.

Michael Billington, *The Guardian*, 22 Nov. 1990

It is a startling play, clearly the work of the author of *The Lower Depths*, and the central responsibility it gives to women is fascinating. . . . Between scenes there are Russian polyphonic chants, sung with surprising power by all the cast. These suggest a faith that Russian humanity will survive both corruption and turmoil.

Alastair Macaulay, *Financial Times*, 20 Nov. 1990

The acting honours go to Lizzie McInnerny, delicately beautiful and unflinching as Rachel, and Paola Dionisotti's Vassa: sardonic, baleful, with sunken cheeks that make her look as if she is feeding upon herself from within.

Using a pleasant translation by Cathy Porter, Katie Mitchell's intelligent production of this forgotten treasure makes lovely use of light. She isolates a pale face against others fractionally darker; or balances one figure, Vassa entering profits in her ledger, against a tight group of all the other characters staring from a doorway. The Russian chants, strongly sung by the cast, are thrilling.

Jeremy Kingston, *The Times*, 20 Nov. 1990

b: Other Plays

*The plays in this section were not published in Gorky's lifetime,
but have been performed.*

Workaholic Slovotekov

Scenario for improvisation.
Written : 1920.
First production: Th. of Popular Comedy, Petrograd, 16 June 1920 (dir.
    Sergei Radlov; des. Valentina Khodasevich; with G. Del'vari as
    Slovotekov).
First published: Arkhiv A. M. Gor'kogo, t. II: p'esy i stsenarii (Moscow,
    1941).

*The scenario begins with the garrulous Slovotekov in bed,
desperately trying not to be woken by his alarm. Defeated, he
crawls out of bed and is interrupted by the arrival of a policeman with news that a water pipe has burst and the road is
flooded. Slovotekov mouths a slogan about co-operative effort
and begins a speech to the policeman. A succession of visitors
bring problems requiring immediate action. His response is a
slogan and an attempt at a political address to each one. The
climax is a rush of political words which seem to spellbind the
listeners: at least, they fall into a deep sleep. Then Slovotekov, too,
runs out of steam and falls on his bed into an exhausted sleep.*

Slovotekov's verbosity is not emphasized . . . [not sufficiently contrasted
with those] who speak . . . and act.

Krasnaia gazeta, 20 June 1920,
quoted in *PSS*, Vol. 19 (Moscow, 1973), p. 534

Radlov directed this piece with enthusiasm. Slovotekov was played by
one of his best performers, the clown Georges Delvari. But the inertia of
the feckless slapstick, which the Radlov actors had already adapted
themselves to, carried them away from satire to farce.

K. Rudnitskii, *Russian and Soviet Theatre*,
tr. Roxane Permar (London, 1988), p. 59

We will not guess what the author wished to say and what his opinion is. Taking everything as it appears to be, however, we should say that Gorky's satirical play *Workaholic Slovotekov* . . . supports the narrow-minded with a mood which smacks of the counter-revolutionary.

V. Chaadaev, *Krasnaia gazeta*, 20 June 1920, quoted in *PSS*, Vol. 19, p. 535

Gorky gave the actors the right to add their own improvizations on topics of the day to the text of the play. *Workaholic Slovotekov* was a fierce lampoon on the type of idler who instead of working holds meetings and makes speeches all the time. In his search for success Del'vari, a clown beloved by the public, forgot his sense of proportion and went over the top at the premiere. His improvisations were so coarse and vulgar that everything turned out to be very unfunny. Radlov and I were terrified and kept looking at the box where leading Leningrad comrades and Aleksei Maksimovich [Gorky] were sitting. It all finished very badly. We were ordered to cancel. . . . Even [Gorky] said that it was possible that he had not fully understood what he had written. . . . I think that some people recognized themselves in Slovotekov and were insulted, and that played a part in the banning of the show.

Valentina Khodasevich, *Novyi Mir*, No. 3 (1968), p. 24

Somov and the Others

A play in four acts.
Written: 1931.
First productions: Volkov Th., Iaroslavl', 1952 (dir. P. P. Vasil'ev; with V. S. Nel'skii as Iaropegov); Sverdlovsk Th., 1952 (dir. V. S. Bitiutskii; des. M. Ulanovskii; with B. Molchanov as Somov and B. F. Il'in as Iaropegov); Th. of the Moscow Council, 1953 (dir. I. S. Anisimova-Vul'f; with R. Ia. Pliatt as Iaropegov).
First published: Arkhiv A. M. Gor'kogo, t. II: p'esy i stsenarii (Moscow, 1941).

This play fictionalizes an actual attempt (the Shakhtinskoe affair) to sabotage Bolshevik power in the late 1920s by representatives of the professional classes. Somov heads a group of engineers who pit themselves against the authorities by sabotaging the local factory. The play is mostly set in Somov's family:

as his political views become clear, so he and his wife Lidiia
become estranged. His views are denounced as fascist. Lidiia
has contacts among the workers and Bolshevik sympathizers in
the local provincial town. Katerina Arseneva, a school friend of
Lidiia and now a teacher, is involved in political work, though
not yet a party member, and provides some romantic interest for
a range of male characters — some Bolshevik and some from
the former gentry class. There are some who are sceptical of
Somov's activities, including Iaropegov, a school friend and
formerly married to his sister, and Troerukov, who sets himself
up as a singing teacher and provides some of the lively comedy.
Crisis gradually approaches as the Bolsheviks discover Somov's
plans from a report by an indignant worker, and Bogomolov, one
of his co-conspirators, attempts to withdraw. The secret police
arrive to arrest Somov and Iaropegov. Bogomolov is also placed
under arrest for being there. To Somov's relief, he suffers a heart
attack: the conspirators feared they might have been incrimin-
ated further by him.

Somov: forty-year-old engineer. Speaks rather stiffly; beneath his restraint there is strong nervous tension. He is sharp, even rude in the
scenes with his mother; he is frank with his wife, indicating his ambition,
not because he is speaking sincerely, but because he is testing himself.

Gorky, notes to the original play, *SS*, Vol. 19, p. 319

V. S. Nel'skii portrayed Iaropegov as a gentle but weak man, much like
a spoilt child in his pranks, and only later reaching a sober evaluation of
himself and his ability to take decisions about his life. B. F. Il'in portrayed Iaropegov as empty, completely eaten up from within by his sceptical attitudes, hostile to most people until events force him to think
about the fate of those around him, and his own fate. R. Ia. Piatt concentrated on the growing crisis in Iaropegov's ironic attitudes.

B. Bialik, *M. Gor'kii: dramaturg* (Moscow, 1977), p. 460

Even though it is unconvincing, *Somov* merits attention for the fact that
of the four plays written by Gorky in the 1930s, during the last stage of
his career, it is the only one that has been set in and reflects the Soviet
period. Exposing once again the spiritual bankruptcy of the Russian
bourgeoisie, it portrays their inability to halt the spread of Soviet power,

their dismay over the 'successes' of the new regime, and their final attempts to turn back history by supporting external intervention aimed at crushing the Soviet state. More important than its trite subject matter and its structural deficiencies is what *Somov* tells us about Gorky's resumption of dramatic writing in the 1930s. . . .

Anxious to demonstrate an ability to deal with Soviet reality . . . Gorky wrote a play about the internal enemies of the new Soviet state and its eventual triumph over them. The play's major redeeming feature is the strong portrait of the titular character, Somov, a forty-year-old engineer with a Napoleonic complex and a fierce hatred of the Soviet regime.

H. Segel, Twentieth-Century Russian Drama
(New York, 1979), p. 29, 30

Surprisingly, Somov and his acquaintances, the villains of the piece, spend so much time on stage that several . . . acquire a certain depth and even grandeur as individuals. The heroes, the true Bolsheviks, by contrast remain shadowy and ill-defined.

B. Scherr, Maxim Gorky (Boston, 1988), p. 97

Iakov Bogomolov

A play in four acts, of which the fourth is unfinished.
Written: 1916-17?
First production: Red Torch Th., Novosibirsk, 1958 (with N. Mikhailov as Bogomolov, and A. Pokidchenko as Vera).
Revived: People's Dramatic Th. of the Construction of the Metro, Moscow, 1960; Central Th. of the Soviet Army, 1962 (dir. B. Erin).
Film: as *A Man Ahead of His Time*, Mosfilm, 1973 (dir. A. Room; with I. Kvasha as Bogomolov and A. Vertinskaia as Ol'ga).
First published: Arkhiv A. M. Gor'kogo, t. II: p'esy i stsenarii (Moscow, 1941).

Iakov Bogomolov, a water engineer, has been engaged by Bukeev to find water on his estate in the South of Russia. Bogomolov and his wife Ol'ga are staying with Bukeev while the work is in progress. Ladygin, a wealthy neighbour, is a frequent visitor. The group is completed by Uncle Jean, Bukeev's former tutor who still clings to his charge, Vera, Bukeev's niece, and Nina, a widowed neighbour. Bogomolov is hardworking, sincere,

*honest, and in love with his wife — all attitudes in direct contrast
to the indolent, careless lifestyle of his host and friends. Ol' ga
enjoys their company, has fallen in love with Ladygin, and is
pursued by Bukeev. The relationship between Ol' ga and
Bogomolov is honest but complex, and she confesses to him,
almost to torture him. There is a row, but they are reconciled.
Ladygin, jealous of Ol' ga's attention to her husband, has taken a
dislike to him. Class as well as emotional antagonisms are
implicit. The play is left unfinished as Ladygin, brooding and
gloomy, idly handles a revolver, and Bukeev, sensing that Ol' ga
is lost to him, announces he is thinking of leaving.*

Attempts were made to persuade dramatists to finish the play for Gorky,
but no one would take on such a difficult task. Then there were attempts
to stage the play in the form it had come down to us. The first attempt of
this kind was made by the Red Torch Theatre of Novosibirsk in 1958.
The theatre prefaced the play with a reading from an article by Gorky on
the poetry of work and creativity. At the end they improvised a scene
without words depicting Ladygin's attempt to shoot Bogomolov. . . .
The Red Torch theatre showed . . . that it was possible to stage this play
about Bogomolov and that the play could deeply engage the spectator.
But this production also demonstrated something else: the more the
spectator was caught up in the play, the more he wanted to ask questions
at the end of it. . . . [In the 1960 production] they did not try to find
means for unravelling the knots tied in the plot, but destroyed them
altogether. . . . All references to an impending crisis were deleted, and a
reconciliation between Bogomolov and his wife provided the ending. . . .
[It became] a play about the difficult love affair of two people . . . not a
Gorky play. . . .

Perhaps it is better not to attempt to finish the play, but to provide a
prologue and an epilogue which would tell the audience that the play
had been found unfinished, and which could describe the possible
variants to its ending?

B. Bialik, *M. Gor'kii: dramaturg* (Moscow, 1977), p. 322-3, 327

Gorky's literary output was large. He moved effortlessly between the short story, the novel, drama, and autobiography. His prose is often referred to as poetic and, although he did not produce a separate collection of poetry, there are numerous instances of poems in his plays and other works. In addition, he engaged in journalistic and publicistic activity, and spent many hours on his voluminous correspondence. All this was from a man who claimed almost no formal education. In the pre-revolutionary period there is an engaging ambivalence in Gorky's plays towards the intelligentsia: on the one hand, he aspires to be a member of it through his writing, while, on the other, he uses his writing to condemn its inactivity and myopic adherence to what he perceives as dying values. In the Soviet period, by contrast, he was made into the model of the perfect proletarian intellectual.

Gorky began his literary career as a short story writer in the 1890s. His first published work, 'Makar Chudra' (1892), has remained one of his most famous. It defined a literary path and reputation which Gorky at first cultivated with sentimental dedication and then, increasingly, with provocative political commitment. Set among gypsies, the tale relates the fate of Radda, the proud heroine, and Loika Zobar, the man who tried to tame her but who even in death could only follow two paces behind. In what appears a deliberate contrast to a famous antecedent, Pushkin's *The Gypsies*, this is a story of jealous passion which ends in the harshness of murder and death, and not in sympathy for an intellectually engaging hero. It asserts an earthy, romantic, folk-framed ethos as Gorky sings with the colourful voice of his people, in his colloquial, florid style and in expression of the primitive but strong mentality of its characters.

Betty Forman argues that Gorky anticipated modern image-makers in his manipulation of his own public reputation.[1] His fame grew with other early stories such as 'Old Isergil' (1894), 'Chelkash' (1895), and the modern fables 'The Tale of the Siskin Who Lied and the Woodpecker Who Loved Truth' (1892) and 'The Song of the Stormy Petrel' (1901). As a result he made his entrance into the literary circles of the capitals in the garb of a man of the people. Chekhov commented on his 'provincialism' as an 'unnecessary dead weight', which caused him to overload his language with too florid and heavy a style, but recognized him as a great artist and representative of a new and necessary voice in Russian literature.[2] That voice, however, also brought a new harshness in its naturalism, derived often from Gorky's youthful experiences of destitution and despair. *Twenty-Six Men and a Girl* (1899), for example, illustrates the grimmer side of Gorky's writing and his relentless attention to the urban working poor. Set below ground in a cellar bakery, the story turns on a bet that the girl, the beloved mascot of the twenty-six, will not sell her body to another worker slightly higher in the bakers' hierarchy. The bet is lost and the despair of the twenty-six at the removal of this one bright spot in their dismal lives is plangent, even tangible.

Many other stories followed, their political implications increasing with Gorky's own leanings towards Marxism and then Bolshevism. As with his plays, the long intervals spent in Italy between 1907 and the First World War, and then again in the 1920s, are reflected in the mellower tone of such works as *Tales of Italy* (1910-13) and *Stories, 1922-1924*.

Gorky turned to the novel with the writing of *Foma Gordeev* in 1899, and, as with his stories, set a pattern that he followed in the majority of his subsequent works. The work is structured on the desire to give as complete a chronicle as possible of the life of the titular character. Themes familiar from the plays emerge, and the characters are similar: generation conflicts, the violence and passion of family life, the dilemma that hard-working, thrusting businessmen of merchant stock face in old age. The novels that follow in the pre-revolutionary period — *The Three of Them* (1901), *The Mother* (1906), *The Life of a Useless Man* (*The Spy*, 1907), *Confession* (1908), *A Summer* (1909), *The Town of Okurov* (1909), *The Life of Matvei Kozhemiakin* (1911) — all fall into a roughly similar category, except for *Mother* and *Confession*. Not only does Gorky write a first 'revolutionary' novel in the former, but he also begins his exploration of motherhood, a motif seen in plays such as *Eccentrics* and *Vassa Zheleznova*.

Mother is, perhaps, the most famous of Gorky's novels, owing to the attention given it by subsequent Soviet and pro-Communist regimes. The growth in political consciousness of the titular heroine, and the activities of the younger heroic revolutionary group engaged in fostering the revolution of 1905, stood as models for the political aesthetic of Socialist Realism. *Confession* is quite different. It poses questions and probes the possibility of a combination of religion and Marxism (referred to as 'god-building') that raised the eyebrows of former associates and endeared Gorky to others who had previously rejected him for his extremist political views.

Two other novels, repeating the chronicle structure, came in the post-revolutionary period: *The Artamanov Business* (1925) and *The Life of Klim Samgin* (1925-36). The first follows the fortunes of a family and the textile business they created from the mid-nineteenth century until the 1917 revolution. The second, unfinished but still claimed by some as

Gorky's masterpiece in the novel form, charts the life of its provincial hero, and also — to some extent mirroring Gorky's own experience — explores his attitudes to the intellectual and revolutionary movement centered in the capitals. It is also a substantial historical chronicle from events of the 1880s through 1905 to the 1917 revolution.

Allied to the novel form, better known, and more obviously written from a personal standpoint is Gorky's autobiographical trilogy. Known in the West through the Soviet films made from them as well as in their translated versions, these three volumes are the true monument to Gorky's narrative skill and to his self-education and struggle for success. They are the hallmark of the 'man of the people' image and ensured him immense credibility within the determining characteristics of Socialist Realism. *Childhood* (1913), *In the World* (1914-16), and *My Universities* (1923) trace Gorky's life into early adulthood, creating unforgettable images of his grandparents, the people who introduced him to Russian literature such as Queen Margot, and the young political activists he mixed with in Kazan'. Despite these companions along his way, Gorky emerges as an isolated, bruised, and reticent individual, interestingly at odds with the confident public image. Some other works proclaim an autobiographical content, notably two collections of stories, *Through Russia* (1915 and 1917) and *Fragments from My Diary* (1924), the latter being retrospective of the period before the revolution, and containing a number of literary portraits of fellow writers such as Tolstoy, Chekhov, and Blok.

One further area of personal reflection is contained in the journalistic activities Gorky undertook at the time of the 1917 revolution. Like his earlier excursion into a form of Marxist Christianity, his *Untimely Thoughts* brought him into conflict with the powers that be. Published in *Novaia zhizn'* (*New Life*), the newspaper of which he was editor between 1917 and 1918, the columns were used to attack some of the more extreme actions of the Bolsheviks, particularly where they affected Russian cultural heritage.

The total body of Gorky's writings — including letters, literary-critical material, reviews, speeches, articles, variants, and unfinished works — filled thirty volumes in the first complete edition published in 1949-56 and thirty-five in 1968-76. There is relatively little of that vast corpus available in English. Much of the critical writing produced in the Soviet period is indigestibly adulatory: Gorky was eulogized as the father of Socialist Realism and fed to generations of Soviet school children in that guise. Probably because of the sheer volume of this material, there has until relatively recently been little western critical writing of note.

We are now doubtless entering a period of reassessment of the Soviet period as a whole. Divested of his Soviet mantle of greatness, Gorky is revealed as an engaging figure who has a great deal to offer the new Russia, and who can act as a bridge from the pre-revolutionary world to the modern one. Tatyana Mamonova, one of the few Russian feminist writers to reach a western public, has already indicated one possible new approach:

I did not discover Maxim Gorky in school, where he was included in the curriculum as a Proletariat writer. . . . In my youth, having swallowed his collected works (in thirty volumes), I dreamt of writing of his feminism. However, as a student at the dogmatic VUZ [an institute of higher education] and after that working in the official culture in Leningrad, I could not imagine such an article being accepted for publication. So now I have returned to this cherished idea in the hope of fulfilling my dream.[3]

Mamonova's article breaks new ground in Gorky scholarship. It waits to be continued and developed. Previously neglected works, particularly the plays between 1907 and 1930, also offer fertile territory for the psychologist of the business-world family. Finally, it is noticeable that almost none of the fictional, autobiographical, or, indeed, dramatic writing makes any direct reference to the Soviet period. Much work remains to be done on the last years when Gorky's real purposes and experiences, possibly obscured by the Soviet propaganda machine, were also the victims of an unprecedented personal reticence.

References

1. Betty Forman, 'The Young Gorky in Russian Literature of the 1890s', *Fifty Years On: Gorky and His Time*, ed. N. Luker (Nottingham, 1987), p. 1-33.

2. A. P. Chekhov, letter to F. P. Batiushkov, 24 Jan. 1900, quoted in F. Holtzman, *The Young Maxim Gorky 1868-1902* (New York: Columbia University Press, 1948), p. 183.

3. Tatyana Mamonova, 'Maxim Gorky: Feminist', *Russian Women's Studies* (Oxford, 1989), p. 55.

a: Primary Sources

Collections of Plays

Details of translations of individual plays are included under their entries in Section 2.

The following collections are available in English:

The Last Plays of Maxim Gorky, adapted by Gibson Cowan, London, 1937. [Contains *Egor Bulichev and the Others* and *Dostigaev and the Others*.]

Seven Plays, tr. Alexander Bakshy and Paul Nathan, New York, 1945; Oxford 1946). [Contains *The Lower Depths*, *Barbarians*, *Enemies*, *Queer People* (*Eccentrics*), the first version of *Vassa Zheleznova*, *The Zykovs*, and *Egor Bulychev and the Others*.]

Selected Works, Volume One: Stories and Plays, Moscow: Foreign Languages Publishing House, 1948. [Contains *The Lower Depths*, *Enemies* (tr. M. Wettlin), and *Egor Bulychev and the Others* (tr. H. Kasanina).]

Five Plays, tr. M. Wettlin, Moscow: Foreign Languages Publishing House, 1956. [Contains *The Petty Bourgeois*, *Philistines*, *The Lower Depths*, *Summerfolk*, *Enemies*, and *Old Man*.]

Collected Works in Ten Volumes, Moscow: Progress Publishers, 1978-82. [Volume Four contains *The Petty Bourgeois (Philistines)*, *The Lower Depths*, *Summerfolk*, *Enemies*, *Egor Bulichev and the Others*, and the second version of *Vassa Zheleznova*.]

Five Plays, tr. Kitty Hunter-Blair and Jeremy Brooks, London: Methuen, 1988. [Contains *The Lower Depths*, *Summerfolk*, *Children of the Sun*, *Barbarians*, and *Enemies*.]

Stories

Through Russia, tr. C. J. Hogarth, London: Dent, 1921.
Best Short Stories, ed. Avrahm Yarmolinsky and Moura Budberg, New York: Grayson, 1947.
In *Selected Works, Volume One* (Moscow, 1948).
Tales of Italy, Moscow: Foreign Languages Publishing House.

Selected Short Stories, tr. B. Isaacs *et al.*, New York: Ungar, 1959.
In *Collected Works, Volume One: Selected Stories* and *Volume Six: Tales of Italy* (Moscow, 1978-82).

Novels

The Three of Them, tr. Alexandra Linden, London: Fisher Unwin, 1902.
The Confession, tr. Rose Strunsky, New York: Frederick A. Stokes, 1916.
The Life of Klim Samgin, tr. Bernard Guerney, New York: Literary Guild, 1930.
The Life of a Useless Man, tr. Moura Budberg, London: Andre Deutsch, 1972. [Also known as *The Spy*.]
In *Collected Works, Volume Two* [*Foma Gordeev*], *Volume Three* [*Mother*], *Volume Five* [*The Life of Matvei Kozhemiakin*], and *Volume Six* [*The Artamanov Affair*] (Moscow, 1978-82).

Autobiography

Fragments from My Diary, tr. Moura Budberg, Harmondsworth: Penguin, 1940.
My Childhood, tr. Ronald Wilks, Harmondsworth: Penguin, 1966.
My Apprenticeship, tr. Ronald Wilks, Harmondsworth: Penguin, 1974.
My Universities, tr. Ronald Wilks, Harmondsworth: Penguin, 1979.
In *Collected Works, Volume Six* [*Childhood*], *Volume Seven* [*My Apprenticeship* and *My Universities*] (Moscow, 1978-82).

Publicistic Works

Untimely Thoughts, tr. Herman Ermolaev, London: Garnstone Press, 1970.

Letters

Letters, tr. V. Dutt, ed. P. Cockerell, Moscow, 1966.
Gorky and His Contemporaries, comp. Galina Belaya, tr. Cynthia Carlile, Moscow: Progress Publishers, 1989. [Contains a selection of literary memoirs about Gorky, and letters written by and to Gorky.]

b: Secondary Literature in English

Background Studies

K. Rudnitskii, tr. Roxane Permar, ed. Lesley Milne, *Russian and Soviet Theatre*, London: Thames and Hudson, 1988. [Magnificently illustrated account of Russian theatre from *c.* 1900 to 1930. Passing references to Gorky, but indispensable to understanding the place of his theatre in this rich context.]

R. Russell, *Russian Drama of the Revolutionary Period*, London: Macmillan, 1988. [Contains references to most of Gorky's plays and their performance. Helpful to the understanding of the political background and how it impinged on theatre.]

M. Slonim, *The Russian Theatre from the Empire to the Soviets*, London: Methuen, 1963. [A standard reference history of the Russian theatre.]

N. Worrall, *Modernism to Realism on the Soviet Stage*, Cambridge University Press, 1989. [Discussion of the work of three major theatre directors, Tairov, Vakhtangov, and Okhlopkov. Contains informative passing references to productions of Gorky's plays.]

Criticism and Biography

F. M. Borras, *Maxim Gorky the Writer: an Interpretation*, Oxford: Clarendon Press, 1967. [Literary-critical approach, sketchy in places, especially on the plays.]

Nina Gourfinkel, *Gorky*, New York: Grove Press, 1960. [Illustrated biography.]

R. Hare, *Maxim Gorky: Romantic Realist and Conservative Revolutionary*, London, Oxford University Press, 1962. [Examines the ambivalence of Gorky's political views. Not primarily literary criticism.]

F. Holtzman, *The Young Maxim Gorky, 1868-1902*, New York: Columbia University Press, 1948. [Scholarly account of Gorky's early life and career. Primary focus is upon his short stories.]

A. Kaun, *Maxim Gorky and His Russia*, New York, 1931; facs. reprint, Benjamin Blom, 1968. [Contemporary biography. Kaun visited Gorky while writing it.]

D. Levin, *Stormy Petrel: the Life and Work of Maxim Gorky*, New York: Appleton-Century, 1965. [Over-romanticized biography with occasional solid comment.]

A Select Bibliography

N. Luker, ed., *Fifty Years On: Gorky and His Time*, Nottingham: Astra Press, 1987. [A selection of articles on Gorky's work, including three on the plays.]

Helen Muchnic, *From Gorky to Pasternak*, New York: Random House, 1961. [Section on Gorky provides a good introduction to his works.]

Alexander Ovcharenko, *Maxim Gorky and the Literary Quests of the Twentieth Century*, Moscow: Sovetskii Pisatel', 1971; tr. Joy Jennings, Moscow: Raduga Publishers, 1985. [Standard, solid work of Soviet criticism by a Gorky scholar, relatively recently translated.]

B. Scherr, *Maxim Gorky*, Boston: Twayne, 1988. [In 'Twayne's World Authors' series. Probably the most useful work on Gorky yet published in English. Within the format of its series, contains good discussion of all of Gorky's creative work, with helpful notes, bibliography, and index.]

H. B. Segel, *Twentieth-Century Russian Drama: from Gorky to the Present*, New York: Columbia University Press, 1979. [The first two chapters contain the most comprehensive discussion of Gorky's drama available in English.]

H. Troyat, tr. Lowell Blair, *Gorky: a Biography*, London: W. H. Allen, 1991. [Readable, fast-moving biography in this writer's series on historical figures.]

For Further Reference

E. W. Clowes, *Maksim Gorky: a Reference Guide*, Boston, Mass.: G. K. Hall, 1987. [Includes both Russian and English sources.]

G. M. Terry, *Maxim Gorky in English: a Bibliography, 1868-1936-1986*, Nottingham: Astra Press, 1986.